The Dream Dictionary

The Dream Dictionary

By:

Carlotta de Barsy

Cover Design: **Gonzales De Santos**
Hori Hashimoto
Layout Editor: **Gonzales De Santos**

Portions Copyright ©2004 by Standard Publications, Inc.
Standard Publications, Inc.
Champaign, IL 61820

All rihgts reserved. No part of this book may be reproduced, stored in a retrieval system, or transmitted, in any form or by any means, electronic, mechanical, photocopying, recording, or otherwise, without prior written permission from the publisher.

The publisher of this book makes no warranty of any kind, express or implied, as to the fitness of this book for any purpose. The publisher shall not be held liable in any event for incidental or consequential damages in connection with, or arising out of, the furnishing, performance, or use of this information.

The publisher offers discounts on this book when ordered in bulk quantities.

ISBN 0-9722691-2-6

Printed in the United States of America

Standard Publications, Incorporated

To The Dreamers Amongst Us!

"A" NOTE

To hear yourself giving out the A note in a concert, is a most favorable omen of success.

ABATTOIR

Dreaming of an abattoir (slaughter house) means illness coming on you; the more blood you see, the graver the illness.

ABSENCE

To see absent persons in your dreams is a sure token of their early return.

ABSINTHE

To drink absinthe in a dream is a sign of complete success; to see a glass filled with absinthe and not to drink it; a bitter disappointment is in store for you.

ACADEMICIANS

To dream of such great lights in the world of literature, science or art, will surely end by headache and dark brooding.

ACCIDENT

To dream of witnessing an accident is a sign of passing worries; to dream that you are the victim of one; slow but final success in your favorite enterprise.

ACCUSATION

If you dream that you are accused of some grave misdeed, it will bring about great delights; if you are the accuser, a deep sorrow awaits you.

ACORNS

When appearing in your dream, acorns mean dire poverty coming.

ACROBATS

To dream of acrobats is a sign of much joy; to see yourself acting the acrobat: many heavy troubles soon coming.

ACTORS OR ACTRESSES

To dream of actors: very complete satisfaction of all your desires; to dream you are yourself an actor (or actress), much anxiety is in store for you.

ADAM AND EVE

To dream of Adam or Eve or both, means an early birth in the family.

ADDITIONS

Adding figures in your dreams is sure to bring you profits in your business or investments.

ADOPTION

If you adopt anyone in your dream, you may depend that most unpleasant troubles are close on your track.

ADULATION

To dream that you are made a great deal of and flattered to the skies, signifies that some of the people that surround you (when you are awake), are cheats and frauds.

ALMONDS

The sight of almonds in dreamland, is a delightful omen of bliss.

ALMS

Distributing alms in your dreams is very lucky; receiving alms is a sign of the worst possible luck in store for you.

ALTAR

To see an altar in a dream betokens a speedy marriage.

AMAZON

A lady on a side-saddle visiting your dreams is a prophecy of endless bickerings between you and your wife.

AMBUSH

To dream of ambush, is a sign of coming worries; on the contrary, to dream that you are actually caught in such an ambuscade, is a prognostic of great success.

ANCHOR

An anchor seen in a dream is a sign of powerful protection extended over you.

ANIMALS

As a general rule, to dream of animals is a lucky omen.

ANTS

There is a general numbness amounting to partial paralysis soon to come over one who dreams of ants.

ANVIL

It is most lucky to dream of a blacksmith's anvil.

APPLAUSE

To listen, in a dream, to sonorous bursts of applause is a sure sign of interested flatterers at work to ruin you.

APPLES

Great profits are promised to one who dreams of apples; but if he sees himself eating apples, he may expect heavy losses.

APRICOTS

To dream that you see or eat apricots promises you plenty of happiness and good health; but if they are dried and it is the season for fresh apricots, losses are threatened.

ARCHBISHOP

To see an archbishop in your dreams is a dread sign of coming death.

ARMY

To dream of an army forebodes a quarrel with those dearest to you.

ARROWS

Temporary sorrows are often announced by arrows appearing in a dream.

ARTICHOKE

To see an artichoke in a dream is a menace of secret troubles; to see yourself eating artichokes is a still worse omen of worries.

ARTILLERY

Cannons seen in your dream announce great profits coming; if you hear them booming, some old relative is about to die.

ASHES

Seen in a dream, ashes announce mourning.

ASIATIC

A man in Asiatic garb appearing in a dream, is an announcement of startling news just about due.

ASPARAGUS

To see asparagus in a dream is lucky; to eat some at the time gives promise of prompt recovery from a disease just then endured by the dreamer.

ATTIC-ROOM

To dream that you see yourself in an attic-room is a threat of poverty.

AUTOMATON

Some such mechanical contrivance, cleverly imitating either man or animal, when seen in a dream announces a great war soon to begin.

AUTOMOBILE

If you dream of seeing a horseless vehicle it means a pleasant visit from an old friend whom you have not seen in years; if riding it, it means an unexpected, tedious journey.

AXE

Seen in a dream, an axe means early violent death.

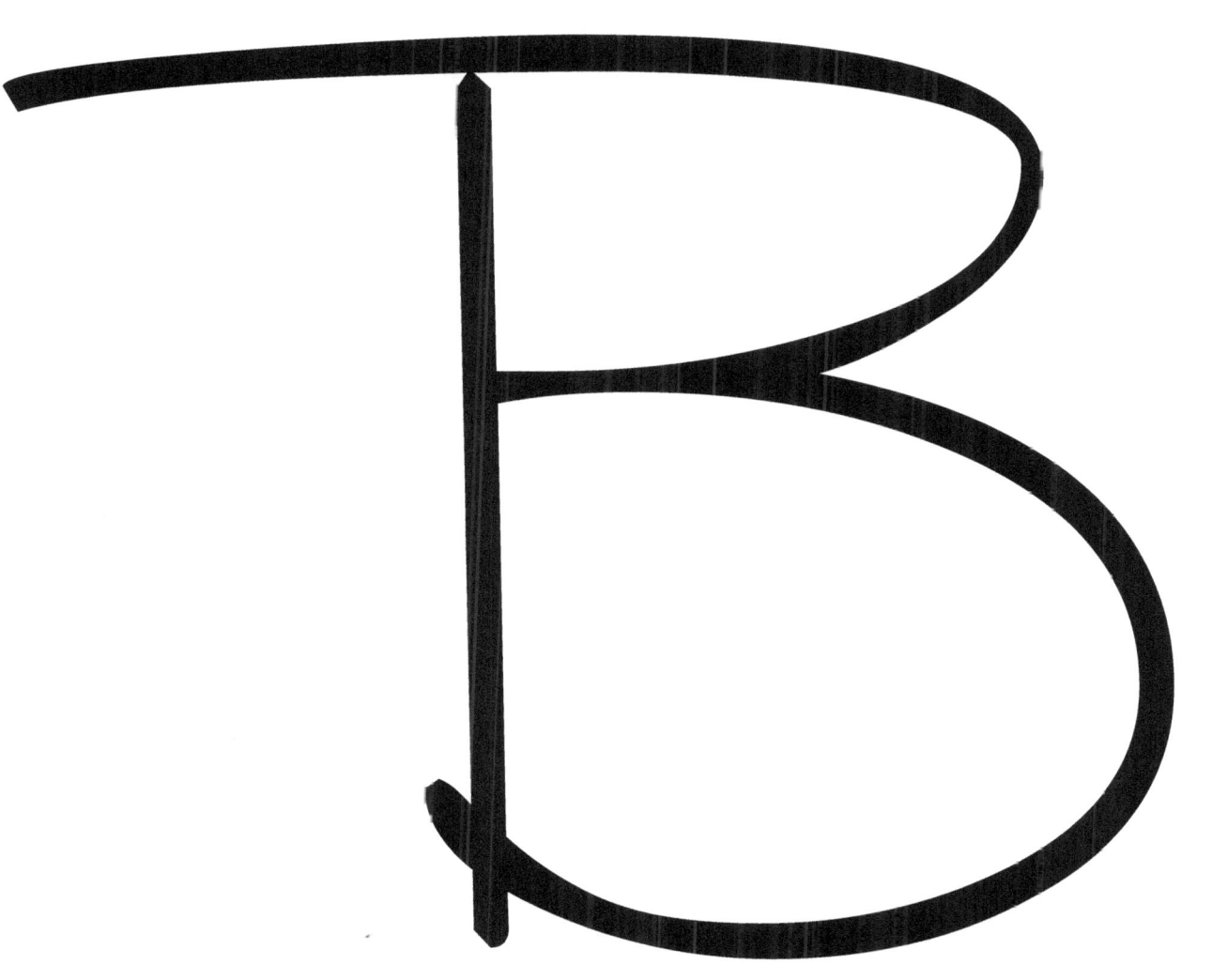

BACKGAMMON

To see yourself, in a dream, playing backgammon means ill-success all around.

BACK

If you see somebody's back or your own in a dream, there is some mischief brewing.

BACON

To see yourself, in a dream, eating or simply cutting a piece of bacon, is a promise of gain.

BAIT

If you dream of fish-bait, some one you love is about to forsake you, causing you bitter sorrow.

BAKER

To dream of a baker is assurance of profits.

BALCONY

Standing on a balcony or even gazing at it, in a dream, is a sure sign of financial ruin; if it should break down while you are on it, sudden death is to be expected very soon.

BALDNESS

To dream of a bald person is a threat of ruin and dishonor.

BALL-PLAYING

If you see yourself, in a dream, playing ball whatever be the game, you may expect in due time a son and heir.

BALL

To dream that you are present at a ball or dancing party, is assurance that your immediate future will be uneventful and quiet.

BALOONING

To dreams of baloons and air-trips is a sure prognostic of great trouble, due to your reckless spirit of adventure or speculation.

BANANAS

To see bananas in a dream is quite lucky; but if you eat any at the time, your sweetheart will most certainly deceive you.

BAND OF MUSIC

To hear a band of music in a dream, means moneyed prosperity and happiness.

BANK

If you dream that you see yourself in a bank, expect to be presently deceived by false promises.

BANKRUPTCY

Anyone dreaming of bankruptcy will find his business growing enormously and prospering apace.

BARLEY

There is prosperity in store for one who sees barley in a dream.

BARN

If an empty barn is seen in a dream, want will soon stare you in the face. But if the barn is full of grain, a season of plenty is forthcoming.

BAR-ROOM OR WINE-SHOP

To see in a dream a liquor-saloon, bar or wine-shop, gives assurance of a long life.

BASIN

Seen in a dream, a full basin means money coming to you; empty, it is a threat of accumulated debts.

BASKET-MAKER

A birth will soon take place in the home of one who sees a basket-maker in his dream.

BATH (COLD)

In a dream, bathing in stagnant, cold water: severe loss threatened; in running water: poor success; in a canal: prosperity.

BATH (WARM)

Dreaming of taking a warm bath, means that the dreamer's marriage is very soon to come off; if the water be too hot. there will be quarrels between the fiancés; if not warm enough, the union will not be a happy one.

BAT

If the repugnant animal called a bat appears in your dream, be certain that illness, money losses, and a painful shock are in store for you.

BAYONETS

Seen in a dream, bayonets are understood as the sign of very serious quarrelling or disagreement.

BEAR

If attacked by a bear in a dream, your enemies will triumph over you; but if the animal runs away from you, expect good success.

BEARD

A very long beard seen in a dream-means an unfortunate undertaking; if it is moderately long and white, honors are to be bestowed, on you; if it is black, luck is in your favor; if a bearded woman appears in your dream, you will soon wed.

BED

In a dream, to see yourself bedridden, means illness coming; but if you are simply resting in the bed, it signifies peace of mind and quiet.

BEE-HIVES

Much happiness and lots of money will come to one who sees bee-hives in a dream.

BEER

To see one's self drinking beer in a dream is a threat of serious trouble.

BEES

Who dreams of bees will reap great profits; if you catch them, success is certain; if they alight on you, many disappointments are to be expected; if they sting you, heavy losses are sure to come.

BEGGAR

There are riches and bliss in store for whoever dreams of beggars.

BELLADONNA

If in a dream, you see or pluck leaves of belladonna (night-shade), or if you drink or make someone drink extract of belladonna, the greatest misfortune will soon overwhelm you.

BELL

If a bell sounds without human agency moving the dapper, it is a sign of death in the family of the person who hears the sound.

BENCH

To sit on a bench, in a dream, gives promise of peace and comfort.

BICYCLE

Many troubles and losses will be the lot of whoever dreams of a bicycle.

BILLIARDS

To see a billiard-table in a dream, is unlucky; to look at one's self playing billiards is a threat of chronic insomnia.

BIN

An empty bin, seen in a dream, meant vorerty; a full bin, prosperity.

BIRTH

There are all kinds of solid comfort promised to one who dreams of a birth.

BIRTHDAY-PRESENTS

To dream that you are giving holiday or birthday presents, means pleasurable surprises coming; if you are receiving them, poverty is in sight.

BISHOP

If you dream of a bishop, one of your near relatives are soon to die.

BITES

To be bitten in a dream is always a sign of great danger ahead.

BLACK-BAT

A person around whom hovers persistently, a black bat, will soon hear news of death.

BLACKBERRIES

To see or eat blackberries in a dream, is an omen of danger and disease.

BLACKBIRD

In a dream, a blackbird announces slander and envy at work against you.

BLADDERS

Who dreams of bladders will meet with cruel humiliations and insults.

BLESSING

To dream that someone is blessing you means that you will soon be forced into very undesirable union.

BLINDNESS

A blind man appearing in you dream, warns you of mendacity on the part of your so-called dearest friends, threatening your happiness. Should you dream of yourself becoming blind, this would prove one of the luckiest signs of all.

BLOOD

If you see blood in your dream, you will soon receive an inheritance. But if you see or feel yourself losing blood, expect great disappointments in the near future.

BOA-CONSTRICTOR

A huge serpent appearing in your dreams is a token of treachery of which you will be the victim.

BOARDING-SCHOOL

If you dream of a boarding-school, a birth will soon be the order of the day in your home.

BOAT

A sailing boat or ship, when dreamed of, announces the arrival of a friend; should it seem in danger of foundering, a severe illness is threatening the dreamer personally.

BOATING-TRIP

To see yourself boating is a warning of treachery.

BOILED BEEF

Eating boiled beef in a dream is a sign of sadness coming; to see yourself boiling it is a joyful token; to throw away some boiled beef is a prognostic of terrible danger ahead.

BONES

In a dream, bones of animals are a threat of financial losses; bones of a human corpse, an omen of death in the family.

BOOKS

To see oneself reading a good book in a dream is a promise of honors and fine position; if you are reading a wicked book, expect nothing but shame and disgrace.

BOOTS (TOP)

There is sorrow coming when you dream of top-boots; if they fit you well, however, prosperity is coming; on the contrary, if they are painfully tight, you may expect ill
treatment and insults.

BOUND

In a dream, to see yourself or someone else all tied up, means that you will soon have to submit humbly to other people's bidding.

BOUQUET

In a dream, to receive a bouquet is a promise of much pleasure coming; if you see yourself giving a bouquet, you may feel sure of your sweetheart's fidelity.

BOW AND ARROW

To see in your dream a bow and arrow forebodes grave misfortune.

BRANCHES

If covered with leaves: branches, seen in a dream, are very lucky; if they are dry, much trouble is in store for you; if you see yourself breaking branches you will suffer from a ruinous robbery or theft.

BRANDY

To dream of brandy tenets the dreamer to many pleasures of a disreputable nature.

BREAD

If you dream of white bread, a delightful friendship is in store for you; if it is brown or black bread, dire poverty is coming.

BREAKFAST OR DINNER

To dream of a meal means that you are about to spend money foolishly.

BRIDGE

To cross a bridge or merely to see one is a threat of danger for the dreamer.

BROOM

Some party or other festivity soon to come is announced to anyone who dreams of a broom.

BROTHER OR SISTER

Dreaming of a deceased brother or sister means long life and prosperity to you.

BUGS OR FLEAS

There are many disgusting troubles ahead for one who dreams of bugs and fleas; but if he sees himself destroying such vermin, he may confidently expect a period of success.

BUILDING-STONE

Many worries will be the lot of one who sees building-stone in a dream.

BULL

Who dreams of a bull will meet with great humiliation, and run serious danger.

BUOY

Seen in a dream, a buoy means danger ahead.

BUSINESS

To dream of your own particular line of work or business is a warning that your salary is shortly to be reduced.

BUTCHER

A butcher-shop or a butcher seen in a dream, warns you of coming ill health.

BUTTER

To see butter in a dream announces surprising news soon forthcoming; and to see yourself churning butter is a promise of inheritance.

BUTTERFLIES

The dreamer who sees butterflies in his sleep, lacks all persistency of purpose; he is very fickle indeed.

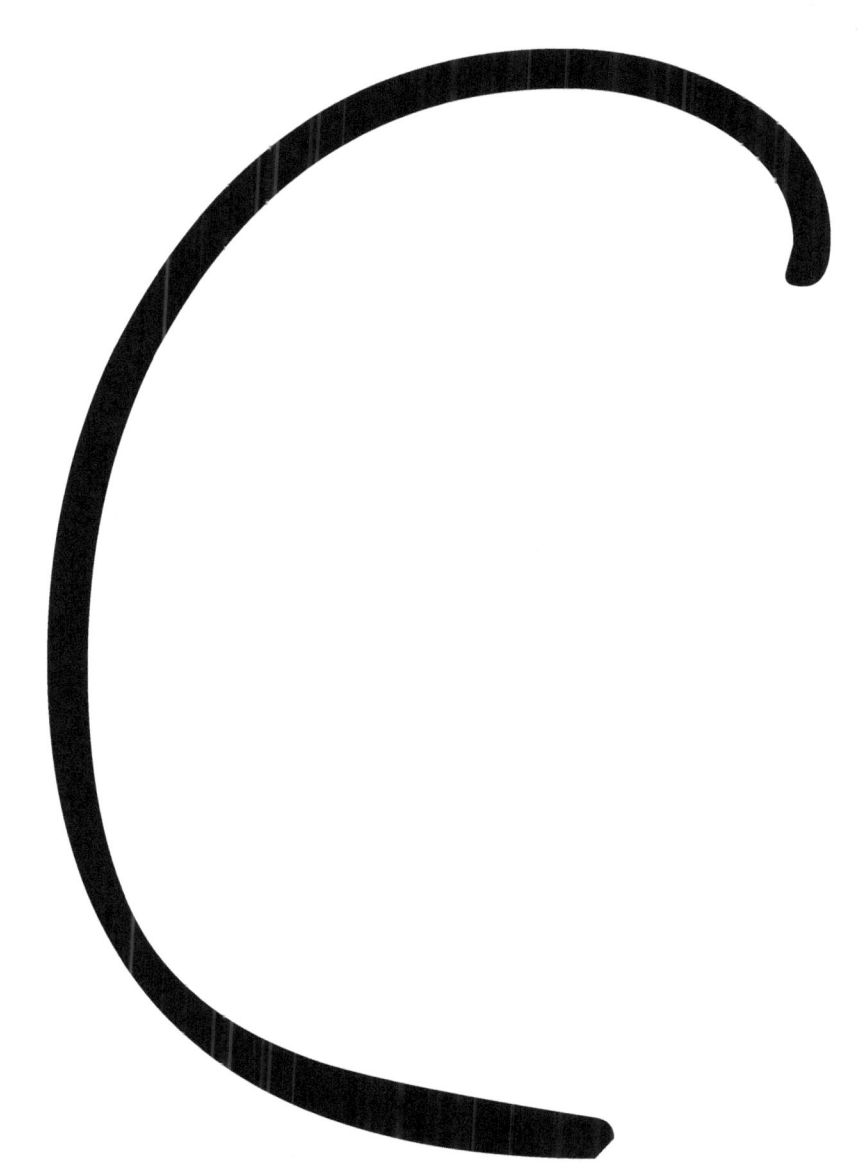

CABBAGE

It is a sign of excellent health and long life to dream of cabbage.

CAGE

To dream of a bird-cage is considered a warning of many treacheries of which you will be the victim.

CAKES

There are many pleasurable moments in store for one who dreams of cakes and pastry.

CALENDAR

To see a calendar or almanac in your dream threatens you with losses in connection with some scandal.

CAMELS

In a dream, a camel is a lucky omen; but if instead of one there is a herd of camels, prosperity will be only fleeting.

CANDLES

If you dream of candles, happiness and prosperity are yours to command.

CANDLESTICK

If you dream of a small hand-candlestick, you are soon to be invited to a wedding.

CANDY

To dream of candy, is a sign of serious money losses.

CANNON

The booming of cannon in a dream announces the death of a close relative; but only to see a piece of ordnance is decidedly lucky.

CAPTIVITY

All forms of captivity we dream of foretell a great deal of quarrelling of the gravest kind.

CARDINAL

To dream of a cardinal is a sign of riches coming; if you see yourself killing such a dignitary of the Church, you will soon suffer from a passing illness.

CARDS

Playing cards in a dream is a sure omen of much disputing.

CARICATURES

If you gaze on caricatures while dreaming, many worries will bother you the next day.

CARPETS

A painful struggle toward success is to be the lot of one who dreams of carpets.

CARRIAGE

In a dream, a carriage means worries and general poor luck.

CARROTS

If you see carrots in your dream, there will be much hard work, anxiety and money tosses in store for you.

CASKS

Barrels or casks, full or empty, appearing in a dream are omens of financial prosperity.

CAT

When a cat puts his paw behind his ear, it means that it is going to rain, and also that a caller will come to you presently.

CATTLE

To dream of horned cattle means plentiful crops; if you see yourself running after them, you will be forsaken, if they run after you, you will soon make a most profitable find.

CAULIFLOWER

In a dream, cauliflower means disease and a woman's deceit.

CAVALCADE

To witness a cavalcade marching past you in a dream, proves that your pride, when awake, is wrongfully assumed; should you see one of the riders unhorsed, there is danger in store for you.

CAVE

To find one's self in a cave, when dreaming, is a sign of great danger ahead.

CELLAR

To witness in a dream an empty cellar, is a promise of excellent health and long life; to see it when full of casks and bottles, assures full and immediate success.

CHAIN

To break a chain in your dream announces some very hard task in store for you; if you simply see one, it is a sign of marriage.

CHAIRS

Your conceit will be humored, but for a short time only, if you dream of chairs.

CHAMELEON

To dream of a chameleon means that you are to be cheated mercilessly.

CHANDELIER

To see a chandelier in a room is an excellent omen of success.

CHECKERS

To play checkers in a dream, means heavy financial losses.

CHECKS

Cashing checks at a bank window in a dream, is a sure sign of loss; if in your dream you pay out money either in cash or by check, this is a token of endless discussions and even law-suits coming.

CHEESE

To dream of cheese gives a promise of final success after a long and hard struggle.

CHERRIES

To eat cherries in a dream denotes a sensual nature; to pick cherries is a prognostic of female fickleness; to see preserved cherries in a glass jar is a threat of unrealized hopes.

CHESS

To see one's self playing a game of chess is a sign of many difficulties resulting from lack of business judgment.

CHESTNUTS

When seen in a dream, chestnuts foretell complete success in one's next undertaking.

CHILBLAINS

To dream of chilblains is an omen of serious troubles.

CHILDREN

To dream of a child, is the promise of one soon to be born; to dream of a pretty child, means pleasure in store, and misfortune coming if he is ugly; if the child you dream of is at play many worries will soon assail you.

CHIMES

There is ill luck and many bickerings in store for one hearing chimes in his dream.

CHOCOLATE

To see or eat chocolate in a dream means coming illness

CHOLERA

To dream of cholera gives one a promise of a bounteous wedding-feast

CHURCH

To dream you see a church means an inheritance coming; if it is being repaired, misfortune is in store for you ; if you enter it repeatedly, delays will worry you greatly ; if you dream that you are shouting in a church, you may expect some serious quarrel.

CHURCHYARD

A dream in which a church yard appears, means a death very close at hand.

CIDER

To see one's self in a dream drinking cider, means some inheritance totally unexpected to come to you shortly.

CIGARS

To see one's self smoking cigars in a dream, or to simply gaze at cigars, is a sign of a very short-lived joy ahead.

CISTERN

Ugly slanders, deeply affecting your reputation, are prophesied by a cistern seen a dream.

CLEANING

To dream of some general cleaning, in house or street, means that you will meet with great ingratitude.

CLOAK

You will soon be cruely cheated if you dream of a cloak.

CLOTHING

A dream in which any kind of clothes play a dominant part, announces sorrows, illness and death.

CLOTS OF BLOOD

To dream that you see clots of blood is a threat of impending quarrels.

CLOUDS

In a dream, the clouds that you see mean so many quarrels.

CLOVER

Four-leaved clover when found accidentally, must be carefully preserved, as it brings luck; when clover stands up in the field, a rainstorm is due.

CLUB OR HEAVY STICK

To dream of a heavy stick is a token of serious quarrel; if, in your dream, you break it, there will be a rupture in the family; if you strike several blows with it, at the time, this is a sign of the warmest friendship about to be shown to you in many ways.

COALS

Dead coals, seen in a dream, mean that you will be the victim of unwarranted jealousy; live coals announce an attack on your honor and good name; if you see yourself eating coals, you will suffer deeply from a secret sorrow.

COCKADE

In a dream, the sight of a cockade means a public insult threatening you.

COCK-FIGHT

It is a sign of stupidity and extreme laziness to dream of a cock-fight.

COFFEE

To see yourself drinking coffee, in a dream, means many disagreeable incidents, and if you are roasting coffee-beans, you will have arduous and ill-requited work ahead of you.

COFFIN

Seen in a dream, a coffin means heavy losses.

COIN

Gold coin seen in a dream, means distress; silver coin, many worries; copper coin, cheating: at your expense.

COLLISION

To witness a collision in your dreams, is a token of great misery and ruin coming.

COMBING

In a dream to see one's self or some one else combing hair with ease, means luck; if the hair is hard to comb, expect difficult times.

COMEDY

To be listening to a comic play in a dream is a sign of peace ahead; if you see yourself just reading such a production, there is a threat of treachery and fraud from which you are to suffer grievously.

CONCERT

To see one's self, in a dream, at a concert, is an omen of pleasure and money coming.

CONJURING

In a dream, to witness conjuring tricks, is a warning of treachery at work to your detriment.

CONTEMPT

When you dream that you are treated with contempt, it means that, after hard struggles, you will finally triumph over your enemies.

CONVENT

To see a convent or a cloister in your dream, is a threat of much sadness and anxiety.

CONVICTS

To dream of convicts is a threat of desperate straits, which you will have to face very soon.

COOKING-POT

Appearing in a dream, a cooking pot means lots of comfort ahead.

COOKING

To see yourself cooking, in dreams, means that there is imminent danger of separation or divorce.

CORDS

Dreaming of cords announces insults to be addressed to the dreamer.

CORPSE

The vision of a corpse in a dream, means sure disaster; if it is already decaying, death will soon overtake you; if the corpse is all dressed up, happiness is in store for you.

CORPULENCE

To see yourself, in a dream, much more corpulent than you really are, is an omen of immoral temptations; if you see yourself thinner instead of stouter, fortune is coming your way.

COTTON-CAP

To see a cotton cap in a dream, warns one of a quarrel between friends.

COTTON-CLOTH

Quick and large profits may confidently be expected after you have dreamed of cotton-cloth.

COUCH

The dream of a couch or sofa is a sign of temporary satisfaction.

COUNTRY

To dream you are staying in the country foretells an unexpected fortune; if you see yourself running towards the open fields, your bliss will be assured and complete; if you are taking a meal in the country, a brilliant match is in store for you.

COUNTRY-BALL

To be present, in a dream, at a popular country ball, is a promise of long life.

COWS

In a dream, cows mean fortune.

CRADLE

A cradle, in a dream, warns you of child's death.

CRAMPS

In a dream, cramps mean an invitation to a dinner or wedding.

CRANE

Utter wickedness on the part of the dreamer is revealed to him when he sees a crane (bird) in his sleep.

CRAWFISH

To see or eat crawfish in dream, is an omen of costly litigation.

CREDITOR

To see one of your creditors in your dream, is a sign of temporary poverty.

CREW

If you see a ship's crew in your dream you are about to start on a long journey.

CRICKETS

These little animals called crickets, seen in a dream, are a prognostic of financial fortune.

CRIPPLED

To see in a dream, one's self or someone else crippled, announces an imminent danger.

CROCODILE

There is much misfortune in store for whoever dreams of a crocodile.

CROSS

To dream that you gaze on a cross, is a sign of a broken engagement; if you see yourself wearing or carrying a cross, you may expect great and valuable assistance when least hoped for.

CROW

It is a sign of great sadness coming, or even of the death of some dear one, to dream of crows.

CROWD

In a dream, to see one's self in a crowd announces a succession of minor worries.

CROWN

A gold crown, in a dream, meant protection of the great; an iron crown, sign of anxiety.

CROWS

To see a crow walking about is a promise of a plentiful harvest. If it is perched, the wheat or corn will be all grass and no grain. It if croaks, you may expect misfortune.

CRUTCHES

In a dream, who sees crutches will soon get lots of money.

CUCKOO

To dream you are hearing the call of a cuckoo is a sign of imminent death and disease.

CURLY HAIR

Much frizzle or curl to a head of hair seen in a dream is a sign of infidelity in the conjugal relations of the dreamer.

CYCLOPS

To dream of a Cyclops (a giant with one eye in the middle of his forehead) is a sign of great profits.

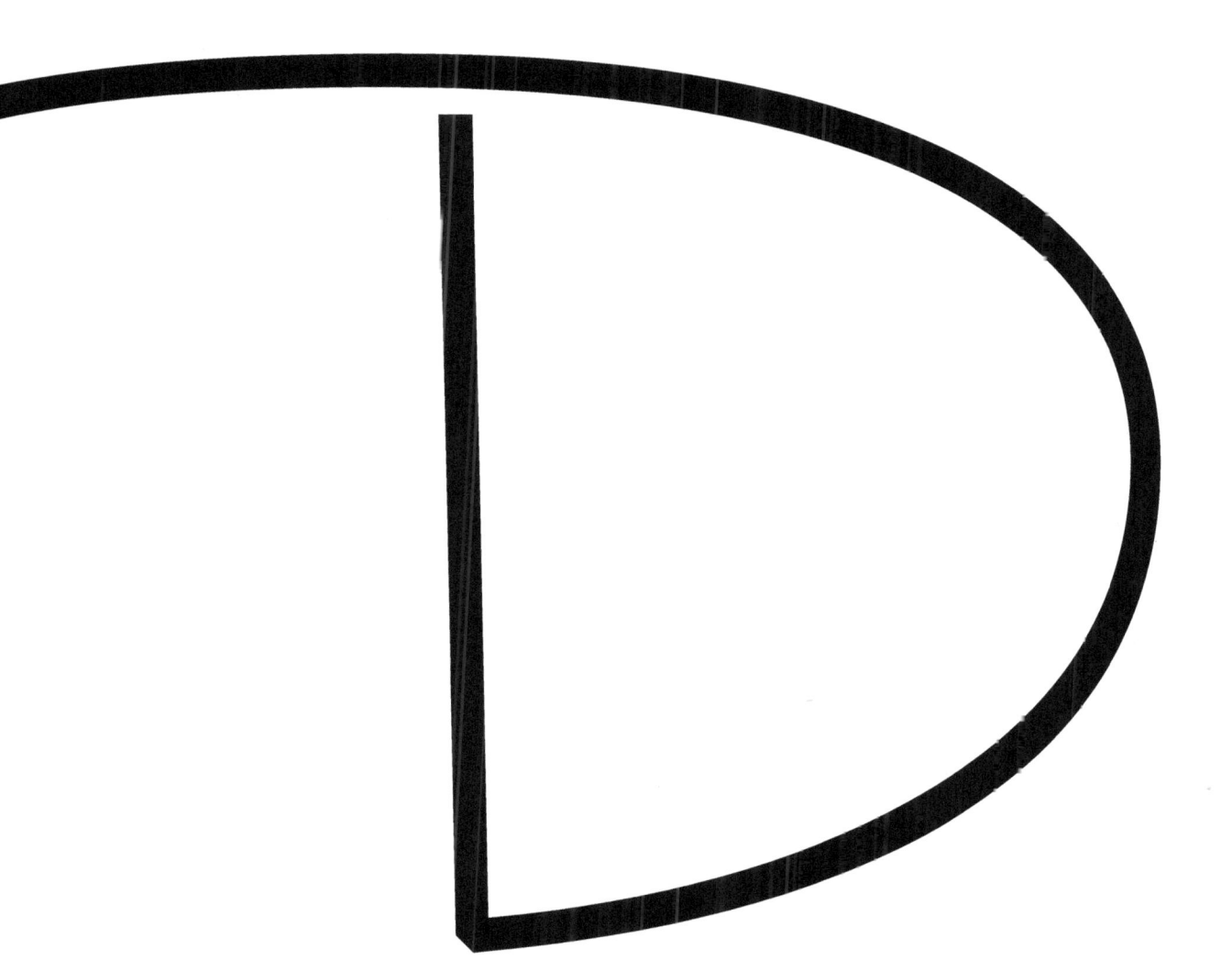

DAGGER

When seen in a dream, a dagger is a sign of misfortune, except you see yourself grasping it firmly; it means then assured success.

DAIS

If you stand, in a dream, under a canopy, or dais, your death is to take place very soon.

DANCING

If you see yourself dancing, in a dream, you are about inheriting a large sum of money; but if you only look on other people dancing, great sadness is in store for you.

DATES

If you see the fruit called date, in dream, you have profits and a good time in sight but if you see yourself eating dates, you will be deceived by some woman you passionately love.

DEATH

Who dreams of death is about to receive some very bad news.

DEBTS

To find one's self, in a dream, settling debts, means that the dreamer will be very hard up for a time.

DEER

In a dream, the apparition of a deer means death, or at least great danger for the dreamer.

DELAY

After blowing once hard upon a dandelion-flower, the maiden who does so will have to wait, before marriage, as many years as there will be feathery petals remaining attached to the flower heart.

DELIRIUM

If you see, in a dream, somebody in the ravings of delirium, many anxieties are in store for you; but if you dream that you are yourself suffering from delirium, you have before you a long life.

DENTIST

If you dream of dentist or dentistry, you will be the object of interested and mendacious flattery.

DESERTER

Whether you dream that you see a deserter, or whether you see yourself desert, in both cases you are just about making a most important discovery.

DEVIL

To dream that you are fighting the devil, indicates a temporary peril; if you conquer him, success is attained; if he conquers you, danger is on the increase; if you only see him in your dream, death is very near indeed.

DIAMONDS

To see diamonds in a dream is a token of short-lived happiness; to see yourself selling diamonds, means great peril ahead; to find diamonds; is a threat of great losses and disappointing merits.

DICE

To be throwing dice in your dream, foretells loss, adversity and deception.

DISINHERITED

To be disinherited in one's dream, means great success coming.

DISTAFF

There is no more favorable omen than to dream of an old-fashioned distaff.

DITCH

In a dream a ditch signify shame, wretchedness and treachery.

DOG

To dream of a setter is a sign of hope ahead; of a rabid dog, a token of great silliness; of a stray dog, a sign of ill-luck; of a barking dog, quarrelling is in store for the dreamer; of dogs fighting, you will have a proof of great enmity or be the victim of a theft; of a howling dog, a terrible misfortune is near; if you dream you are bitten by a dog, it is a sign of mere temporary trouble; if the animal caresses you, you have a true friend coming to your assistance. Summing up: dog dreams are generally favorable.

DOG-BARK

To dream that you hear a dog barking, foretells quarrels and bickerings.

DOLMAN

Seen in a dream, a dolman means honesty and courage displayed by the dreamer.

DOME

If a lofty dome arise before your dreaming eyes, some enemy is at work against you.

DOOR

To dream of a door is a sign of worries a and sorrow; to gaze upon a broken door is an omen of death.

DOUGH

Whoever dreams of dough or of kneading dough, will soon enjoy a general improvement, physical, mental and financial.

DOWN

To dream of soft, fleecy down, means friendship helping one to success; if the down is black colored, there is a loss in sight.

DRAWING

To dream of a drawing or sketch, announces worries; if the dreamer is doing the drawing himself, he is threatened with serious losses.

DREAMS

To dream that you are dreaming means that you will soon be cruelly deceived and cheated.

DREGS

If you dream of dregs of any kind, expect poverty and loss of position.

DROMEDARY

To see in a dream a one-hump camel, called a dromedary, is an excellent omen of fortune and success.

DRUGGIST

To dream of a druggist means that a baby is coming to visit you.

DUEL

To witness one's self fighting a duel means that a favorite pleasure you expected to enjoy will not be granted you.

DUMBNESS

To dream of a dumb person announces the birth of a deformed or afflicted child.

DUNG-HILL

There are great profits in sight for whoever dreams of dung or dunghill.

DWARF

It is an omen of hatred against which you had better protect yourself, to dream of a dwarf.

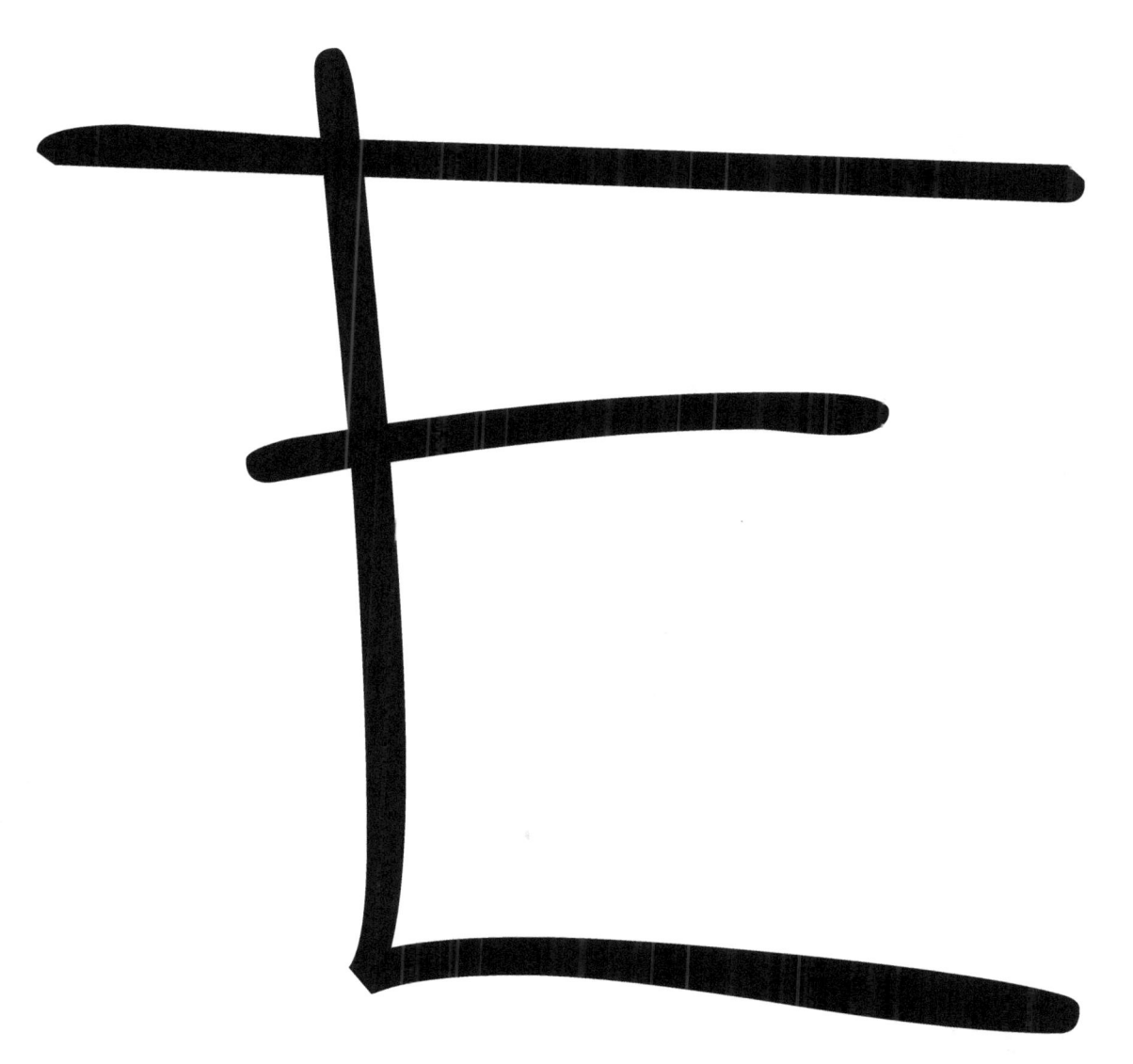

EAGLE

To dream that you are killing an eagle, success in your most cherished ambitions; that you are eating its flesh, the deepest grief awaits you; that you see an eagle soaring in his glory means that your ambition and conceit are boundless.

EARS

Well made ears, seen in a dream, give promise of valuable friendship; too large, they are evidence of low instincts in the dreamer; if they are dirty, of a thieving disposition; if they are cut off, of treachery at work. Ears of animals seen in a dream may be interpreted as above.

EARTHQUAKE

There is great peril in store, in the immediate future, for one who dreams of earthquake.

EATING

In a dream to see yourself or someone else eating, means that traitors are encompassing your ruin.

ECHO

To hear an echo in your dream, announces illness coming.

ECLIPSE

An eclipse of the moon, if witnessed in a dream, means sorrow in store for the dreamer; an eclipse of the sun, a loss of money and ill-success in general.

EEL

To dream of a live eel means hard work ahead; of a dead eel, triumphant success in all one's undertakings.

EGGS

In a dream, to see or eat eggs is omen of fortune; if you see broken eggs, there are losses ahead.

ELEPHANT

To dream you are riding an elephant is a sign of a preposterous vanity that will cause you lots of trouble; if you just see one, that's good luck coming; if you face an elephant in your dream, you will render someone a service that will be returned to you tenfold.

ELOPEMENT

To dream that you are eloping with someone is a sure omen of a marriage set to take place.

EMBROIDERY

One who dreams of lace embroidery is extremely ambitious, but will fail.

EMPRESS

Dreaming of an empress means duplicity at work to ruin you.

ENEMY

To dream that you meet an enemy and converse with him is an omen of ruin and disaster; if you see yourself triumphing over him, you are about winning a law-suit; if you dream that you are having a pleasant time with him, you may expect great troubles due to your thoughtless confidence.

ENGAGEMENT

Being engaged, in a dream, to a handsome man (or woman), means great pleasures forthcoming; if the person to whom you are thus engaged is plain-looking, many worries or even griefs are in store for you.

EWE-SHEEP

To dream of a ewe is a sign of a faithful, precious friendship; if the animal you see seems ill, it is a token that a period of great fatigue is in store for you.

EXECUTION

To see yourself, in a dream, about to be hanged or beheaded, is a sign of the greatest luck coming; to dream of another in the same predicament, is a token of the unfaithfulness of someone very dear to you.

EXHUMATION

To dream about the disinterring a human being is an omen of disaster; if you see yourself exhuming the remains of a dead person, there is treason surrounding you.

EXILE

To dream that you are going into exile, is a highly favorable omen; but to see yourself, in your dream, returning from exile, means great sorrow coming.

EXPLOSION

To hear an explosion in a dream is a threat of death in the family.

EYEBROWS

If, in your dreams, eyebrows are particularly noticeable, you may expect terrible events and even death.

EYES

Dreams about eyes are generally omens of good luck; the prettier, the dearer, the purer the eyes, the better the luck; if they show signs of illness, some temporary troubles will soon assail the dreamer.

FAINTING-FIT

To dream that you faint, or that you see someone fainting, is a sign of true love coming to you.

FALCON

There is fortune and bliss in store for one who sees a falcon in his dream.

FALL

To feel one's self falling, in a dream, is a threat of grievous troubles and losses.

FAN

In a dream, the vision of a fan means quarrelling.

FARM

To gaze upon a farm in a dream is a promise of success and riches.

FATHER

To dream of your father alive is a promise of great joy; to see him dead announces heavy financial losses.

FEATHER

In a dream, white feathers are in omen of success; dark feathers, just the reverse.

FEET

In a dream, a vision of feet means journey in the near future; if they are dirty or wounded, you may expect illness, sorrows, and losses.

FENCING

To dream that you are using fencing-foils is a most favorable omen.

FERRET

Seen in a dream, a ferret is an omen of luck.

FERRY-BOAT

News from a near relative is the prognostication of a dream about a ferry-boat.

FEVER

There is a sign of excesses committed out of sheer stupidity by the dreamer, when dreams that he is passing through a spell of fever.

FIGHT

In a dream, a fight means peace.

FIGS

To see green figs in a dream is a hopeful omen; if they are dried, you will shortly be invited to a state dinner; if you see yourself eating figs of any land, poverty will soon overtake you.

FIGURES

To dream of figures or numbers is a threat of fraud you are to be made the victim of.

FINGER-NAILS

There are few worse omens than nails seen in a dream; they mean suffering, sorrows and quarrels.

FINGERS

To cut one's fingers in a dream is a sign that you are about to lose a friend on account of a serious disagreement; if you see yourself with more fingers than the normal number, your marriage will be a failure.

FIRE

To dream of a small fire means pleasures are in store; if it is a large conflagration, some great festivity is soon to come off; if a fire is slow starting, sincere love will soon come to you; if starts suddenly, there is a threat of quarrelling; you dream you are touching fire without burning yourself, success is yours; but if you are burned in the act, you will meet with great disappointment and failure.

FIREWORKS

A birth is often announced by brilliant fireworks seen in a dream.

FISH

Live white or red fish in a dream means success; to see dead fish is a prognostic of worries, disputing, and even death.

FISH-HOOKS

In a dream, fish-hooks are a sign of treason.

FISHING

You will soon be deserted and in trouble if, in a dream, you see yourself fishing.

FLAG-STONES

If you dream of flag-stones, beware of the treachery of so-called friends.

FLAMES

Brilliant flames seen in a dream prognosticate some fine festivity soon forthcoming.

FLEET

To dream of a fleet of men-of-war is a sore promise of the fullest realization of your hopes.

FLIES

In a dream, flies mean rivalries and jealousies.

FLIGHT

To dream one is running away is a token of catastrophe.

FLOOD

To dream of a flood is a threat of a slanderous attack upon your reputation.

FLOUNDERS

To dream of the fish called flounders is a sign of dire poverty coming.

FLOUR

There are riches promised for those who dreams of flour.

FLOWERS

To dream you see flowers is the sign of a valuable friendship; if you are wearing them, you will soon be married; if you are throwing them away, worries await you; if you tear them to pieces, a sure sign of divorce; if you pluck them, a token of good health.

FLUTE

Should you hear a flute in dreams, there will be a birth in the house.

FODDER

A dream in which some kind fodder appears, is a sign of prosperity coming

FOILS

To see fencing-foils in a dream is a threat of mishap; to see one's self using one of them is a very lucky omen.

FOREHEAD

A low forehead seen in a dream means stupidity on the part of the dreamer; a high one, intelligence; one almost covered with hair, some bitter hatred at work against the dreamer; a white and unwrinkled brow, an unclouded future in sight.

FOREST

Appearing in a dream, a forest wood announces dire anxiety and heavy losses.

FORGE

To dream of a forge in operation, means that through hard work you will succeed brilliantly.

FORK

A pitch-fork or table-fork seen in a dream, means that you are about to be the victim of some wicked intrigue.

FORSAKING

If you dream that you are forsaking your wife or husband, it means great joys in store for you; if you are forsaking of changing your occupation, somebody's dishonesty will cause you a heavy loss. If you dream that you are abandoning your home, your business is to grow more and more profitable.

FORT

To see a fort or fortress in your dream is a threat of a lawsuit and prison.

FORTUNE-TELLING

To dream that you are having your fortune told is a token of a lot cruel gossip, slander and calumny that will render life a burden to the dreamer.

FOUNTAIN

A clear, limpid fountain means excellent health and all the comforts of life; if the water is muddy, many grievous worries await you.

FOX

To dream of a fox is a warning of some treachery awaiting you; to kill one means luck ahead.

FRIEND

To dream of a friend alive means pleasure ahead; to see yourself having a good time with him is a sure omen of trouble ahead; to see him dead means financial worries to assail you very soon.

FRITTERS

To dream that you see or eat fritters of any kind is a promise of good times.

FROGS

Trouble, illness, and disappointments through false friends, are foretold by frogs seen or heard in a dream.

FROST

If, in your dream, you see the evidence of frost, you have therein a strong assurance of success.

FRUIT

To dream of fruit is a promise of profit and pleasures. To eat fruit is a threat of feminine deceit; to throw away fruit in a dream prognosticates some imminent calamity.

FUNERAL

To dream of a funeral means a marriage in the immediate future; to dream you see yourself or some one else buried alive, is a promise of a large inheritance.

FURS

There is a promise of comfortable security in a vision of furs, in a dream.

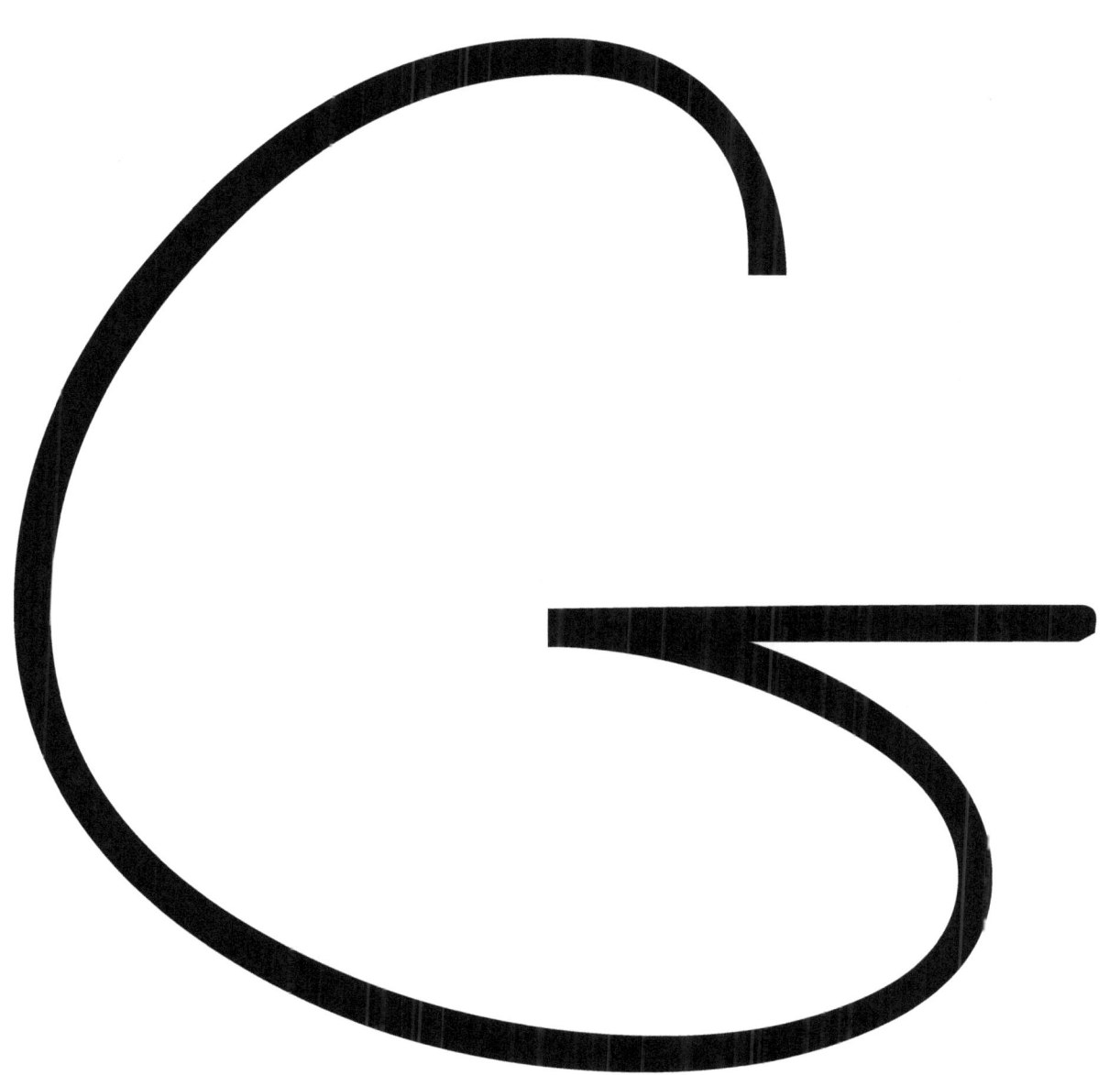

GAFF

To dream of a gaff, or boat-hook, means that you will soon be the victim of a dangerous set of plotters.

GALLOWS

To dream of a gallows or of someone being hanged, is a terrible omen of disaster and death.

GAMBLER

A gambler or a gambling house seen in a dream, always signifies treachery surrounding you.

GAMES

When played in a dream, all games are disastrous omens.

GAME

There is pleasurable comfort in store for you if you dream of game.

GANGRENE

To dream of mortification of gangrene setting in is a threat of a painful separation.

GARBAGE

To see or sweep garbage is a threat of coming separation or divorce.

GARDEN

A well kept garden promises the dreamer pleasure and profits; an ill-kept one, is an omen of ruin.

GARLIC

The taste of garlic in your dream, threatens you with the treason of your best loved one.

GARRET

In a dream, to see or find one's self en a garret is a highly favorable omen.

GARTERS

Who sees garters in his dream may expect an illness in the near future.

GAUZE

To dream of that airy tissue named gauze is to be notified of some hypocrisy at work against you.

GEESE

To dream about geese is an assurance of joy and luck ahead.

GIANT

In a dream, a giant means sudden good fortune.

GIRDLE

To dream that you see a girdle means that your marriage will very soon take place; if the girdle is green or blue your happiness is assured; if it is made of gold or silver, great worries will make your life a burden.

GLOVES

It is a very unlucky omen to dream of gloves.

GOAT

If you dream of a billy-goat, you health will be poor; if you only see its horns, war will stare you in the face; but if, in your dream, you or someone else kills the animal, luck is on you side.

GOBLET

To dream of a goblet is a sign of exaggerated conceit on the part of the dreamer.

GOSSIP

To hear a lot of gossip, in your dream, promises you some small profit.

GOUT

To feel a twinge of the gout in your dream, is evidence of your laziness and apathy in matters of importance.

GRAND-PARENTS

To dream of grand-parents is a harbinger of inheritance.

GRAPES

Much joy and large profits are promised to one who dreams of grapes.

GRASSHOPPERS

To dream of grasshoppers prognosticates a wretched future and great poverty due to a lack of energy on the part of the dreamer.

GRASS

To see grass in a dream, is a prognostic of fortune.

GREYHOUND

Seen in a dream, a greyhound is evidence of silly, improvident and extravagant habits on the part of the dreamer.

GUDGEONS

To dream that you see gudgeons, a sign of success; that you are catching the omen of betrayal of a trusted one.

GUILLOTINE

In a dream, the fatal instrument called a ""guillotine"" is a promise of great fortune.

HAIL

To see or hear hail falling in a dream is a threat of worries.

HAIR

When dreaming of hair: if it is white, high honors are soon to be bestowed upon you; if it is blonde, a friendship will stand by you; if it is black, a threat of terrible misfortune; if it is a mixture of two colors, an omen of separation or divorce; if you dream that you are holding cut-hair in your hand, your revenge will be fully accomplished.

HAIRDRESSER

The appearance of a hairdresser in your dream foretells some festivity soon to take place.

HALL

If you dream of yourself in a large hall, there are great profits coming to you. If it is the Hall of Congress, you may expect treachery from those you believe your best friends.

HAM

There is a sign of large profits in a dream wherein hams are prominent.

HAMMER

Much wretchedness and poverty it in store for one who dreams of a hammer.

HANDCUFFS

To see yourself with handcuffs or simply to see them lying about is a warning of the gravest business difficulties ahead.

HANDS

In a dream, to see hands means, if they are white, large profits; if they are dirty, a thief at your expense; if they are thick and heavy, a valuable friendship; if they are entwined, someone faithful devotion; if they are cut at the wrist, your ruin is to be completed in the near future. Finally, if you dream that you are washing your hands, large fortune will soon come to you.

HANGINGS

Any kind of hangings conspicuous in a dream, mean that the pleasures in store for you will be deceiving in every way.

HAREM

There are lots of pleasure ahead for the one who dreams of a harem.

HARE

To dream of a dead hare, is a most favorable omen; but if you dream that he is running away from you, you will surely run into debt, the consequence of your spendthrift ways.

HARNESS

To dream of a harness means that you will very soon start on a journey.

HARPOON

Whoever dreams of harpoons will be beset by intrigues and treachery.

HARVEST

To witness or take part in a harvest is a sign of prosperity.

HAWTHORN

To tie a sprig of hawthorn to a new-born baby's cradle will bring the child good luck.

HAY

To see hay in a dream is a favorable sign; to see one's self cutting hay announces a sorrow coming.

HEAD

To dream of a head, even if it is cut off, may be an assurance of plenty of luck, health and money; but if the head is ugly or repulsively dirty, the dreamer may expect the worst kind of worries.

HEADGEAR

Any kind of hat or bonnet, for male or female use, if seen in a dream, is a sign of betrayal on the part of your husband (or wife).

HEARSE

Seen in a dream, a hearse signifies sorrow and loss.

HEDGE-HOG

Many business troubles will assail one who dreams of hedge-hogs.

HENS

Merely to see hens in a dream is quite lucky; but to see yourself killing hens or chickens is a warning of disaster.

HERRING

To dream of fresh herring means success; of red herring, trouble.

HIPPODROME

To dream of a circus ring or hippodrome is a most favorable prognostic.

HIPS

Well proportioned hips seen in a dream are a promise of happiness; if they are too narrow, there is divorce and even death in store for you; if they are too broad, you are threatened with a fatal disease; if they are wounded, there will be serious trouble in your home.

HOLD-UP

If you dream you are waylaid or held up, you may expect many serious troubles in the immediate future.

HOLE

In a dream, to gaze at a hole or, worse, to fall into it, is an omen of death.

HONEY

Plenty of money is in store for you if you dream of honey.

HOOKS-AND-EYES

Hooks-and-eyes, in dreams, are to be interpreted as announcing varied pleasures of the most charming nature.

HOOTING

To be hissed and hooted, in ones dream, is a sign of coming worries.

HORNS

To see horns on one's forehead, in a dream, means treason on the part of the dreamer's sweetheart.

HORSEBACK-RIDERS

Riders, of either sex, seen in a dream, reveal the extreme vanity the dreamer.

HORSE-SHOE

To see one's self, in a dream, picking up a horse-shoe, is very lucky; if you simply see one, a journey will soon be undertaken by you.

HORSE-TRADERS

To dream of horse-traders or horse-trading, is a sign that you are about to be cruelly cheated.

HORSE-TROUGH

To dream of a horse-trough filled with clear water, an excellent omen; filled with dirty water, grave troubles ahead.

HOSPITAL

Seen in a dream, a hospital means extreme want.

HOTEL

To see a hotel is a sign of imminent departure on a journey.

HOUSE

To dream of a house signifies profits; if it has been burned, there is fortune with honor in store for the dreamer; if you see yourself building it, you will enjoy but a deceptive pleasure; if, instead, you are having it pulled down, your undoing is a matter of a short time.

HOWLING

To hear howls in a dream is an omen of death.

HUGGING

To dream that you are either hugged or hugging means that some nasty trick is about to be played on you by a pretend friend.

HUNGER

To feel the pangs of hunger, in dream, is a very lucky omen.

HUNTING

To see yourself in a dream, going out shooting or hunting is the omen of a death among your nearest friends; but if you see yourself coming back from such an expedition, there is excellent health in store for you.

HUNTING-HORN

To dream of a hunting horn is a threat of dishonor; if you hear yourself playing it, you will surely receive a heavy sentence in court.

HYDROPHOBIA

Any animal affected with rabies, appearing in a dream means that the dreamer will suffer grievously through his own stupidity.

HYENA

Seen in a dream, a hyena is a threat of a cruel sorrow coming.

HYMNS

The singing of hymns in a dream announces the death of the dreamer.

HYPOCRITE

To see a hypocritical fellow in a dream is a warning of some treachery at work against you.

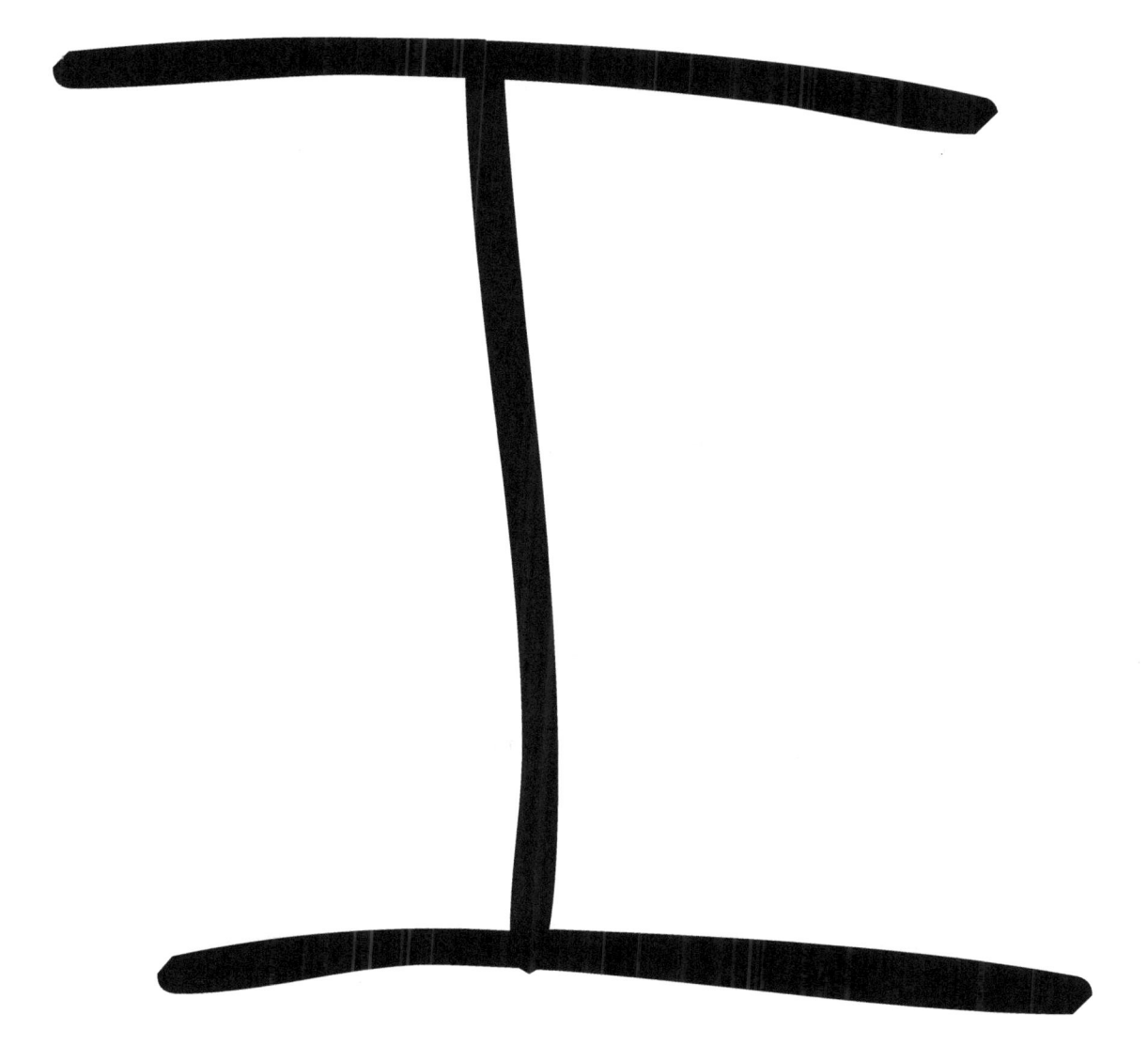

ICE

Who dreams of ice or ice-cold water is sure to meet with success.

IDIOT

There is a serious grief in store for you. if you dream of one of those benighted being railed natural idiots.

IDOLS

Anxieties will torment one with dreams of idols.

ILLNESS

To dream of disease is a warning danger.

IMPRISONMENT

Perfect happiness is coming to one who sees himself in his dream behind prison-bars.

INFIRMITIES

To dream of old age's infirmities is an assurance that you will live to a green old age.

INHERITANCE

To dream of an inheritance is an omen of some near relative's early death

INK

To spill ink in a dream is a threat of broken engagement; but dreaming of ink in any other way is a favorable omen.

INSANITY

To dream of insanity or of some insane person, is an omen of great trouble; to see yourself becoming insane, is an excellent promise of long life.

INTOXICATION

Intoxication indulged in or gazed upon in a dream, is a favorable sign; if it is beastly and brutal, it is a warning of most terrible retribution.

INUNDATION

There is sadness, loss of courage and illness for one who sees an inundation in his dream.

INVECTIVES

One who hears invectives and insults addressed to him in a dream, may count upon a long spell of enjoyment.

IRON

Simply to see some iron in a dream means profits; but if it is burning hot, sorrows are forthcoming.

ISLAND

To see an island in a dream foretells that the dreamer will be wantonly forsaken.

ITCH

To dream that you are afflicted with "the itch" is one of the most favorable omens you may desire.

ITCHING

If you suffer from some other sort of itching, in your dream, you will surely meet will misfortune.

IVY

Seen in a dream ivy means strong trust worthy friendship in store for the dreamer.

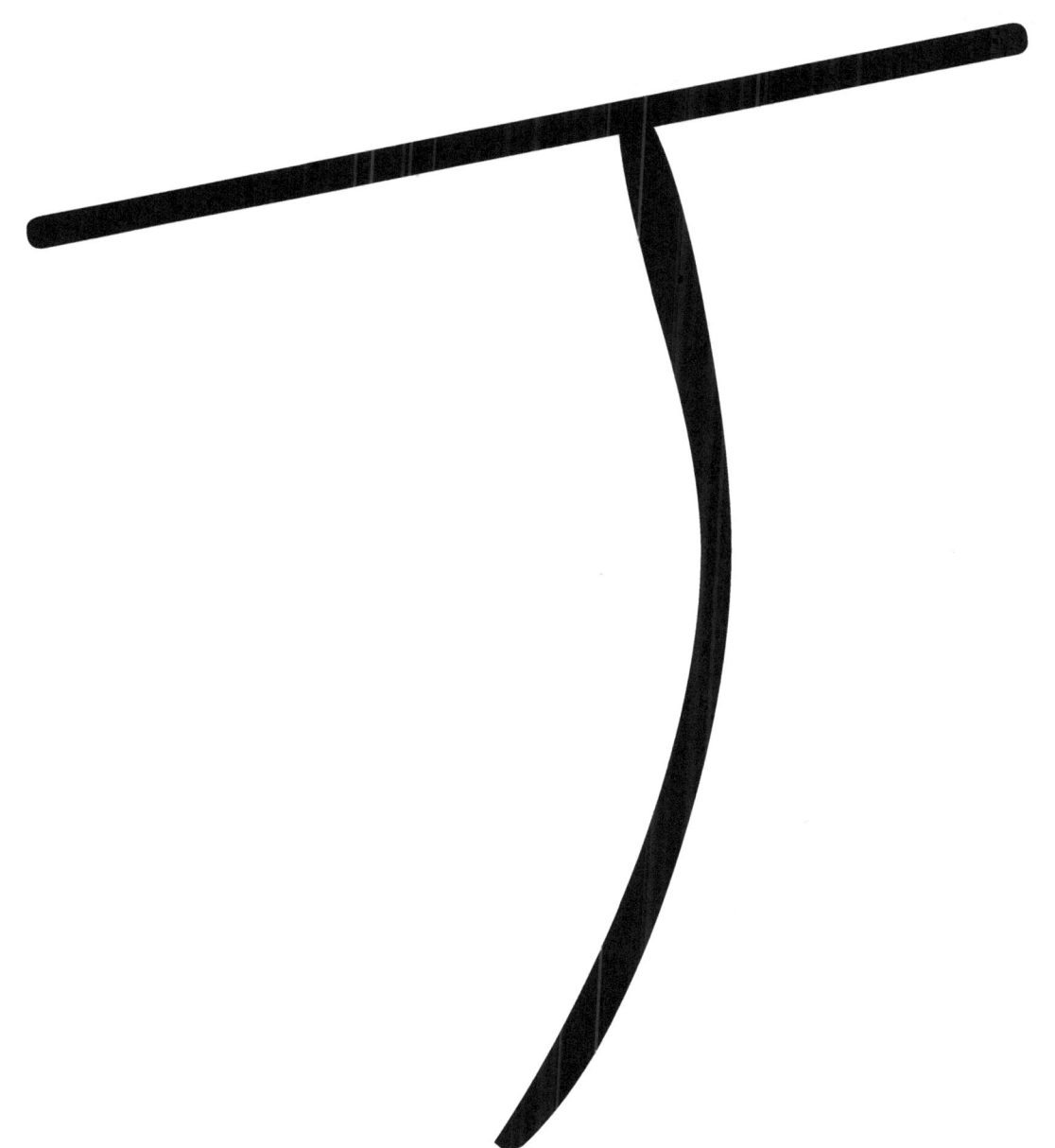

JAM

To dream of jam or preserves is a threat of financial losses.

JANITOR

Appearing in a dream, a janitor always signifies gossip of the worst kind about to ruin your happiness.

JAUNDICE

To dream about jaundice is warning of treachery at work to ruin you.

JAVELINS

Temporary troubles must be expected by one who dreams of javelins, shafts, or spears.

JAWS

There is a sign of illness for anyone dreaming of jaws.

JAY

Who sees a jay-bird in his dream will awake to find many new cares awaiting him.

JEWELRY

There are many cares and no little danger in store for one who dreams of jewelry.

JUDGE

A dream about a judge signifies that you are surrounded by intrigue, opposition and ill-feeling.

JUG

In a dream to see a jug very prominent is an omen of loss due to a fault of judgment on your part or that of an intimate friend or relative.

KANGAROO

A kangaroo in a dream announces prolonged worries; but if you see yourself killing one, you will meet with a streak of luck.

KEYS

A vision of keys, in a dream, means many worries and very narrow means to live on.

KILLING

If you see yourself killing someone in a dream, you will be sure to meet, very shortly, with disaster and even death.

KING OR EMPEROR

To see yourself in a dream a King or an Emperor means that you are soon to be made the victim of impudent flatterers.

KIOSK

To see in a dream an elegant little pavilion known as a kiosk is a sign of peace and plenty; but if you gaze upon yourself building one, there will certainly be trouble between you and your sweetheart.

KISSES

There are many meanings given to kisses bestowed in a dream; here are the leading ones: According to the Hindus: Kissing someone in a dream out of mere affection, is a sign that you will be his (or her) benefactor: if you give him or her a real love-kiss, you will be yourself the recipient of the benefits. If you kiss on the neck: great happiness is in store for the one you kiss. If the kiss is given on the shoulder, you will be highly thought of as person of the other sex; if given on the arm, your benefactor will be a brother or close friend. If you dream you are kissing a beloved one already dead but alive in your dream, his or her heirs will do you a great kindness. According to the Persians and Egyptians: If you dream that you are kissing a sworn enemy hoping to conciliate him (or her), the misunderstanding will grow still more bitter. If the person thus kissed is not a real enemy, your kissing him means that he will soon reveal to you weighty secrets. Kissing one who is dead is a sign of great sorrow. Hugging a horse or a donkey or a mule in a dream means happiness and prosperity your life long. Hugging a monkey in your dream is a warning to beware of a dangerous enemy who makes a great show of being devoted to you. Kissing a near relative, promises you his gratitude in proportion to the pleasure and enthusiasm you put in your dream-kiss.

KITE

There is a lawsuit coming when you dream of a kite.

KNIFE-GRINDER

To hear or see a knife-grinder in passing or at work is an omen of a heavy loss at cards or in some speculation.

KNITTING

To dream of knitting is the omen of much silly gossip hurting your prospects or station.

KNIVES

Disagreement between friends will surely follow a vision of knives in a dream. Should they be crossed, death will ensue. If a knife wounds you in a dream, it is a sign of murder.

KNOTS

Endless money difficulties will be the lot of one who dreams of knots.

KNOUT

To see one's self in a thrashed with the terrible Russian whip called "Knout" is a threat of home-quarrels.

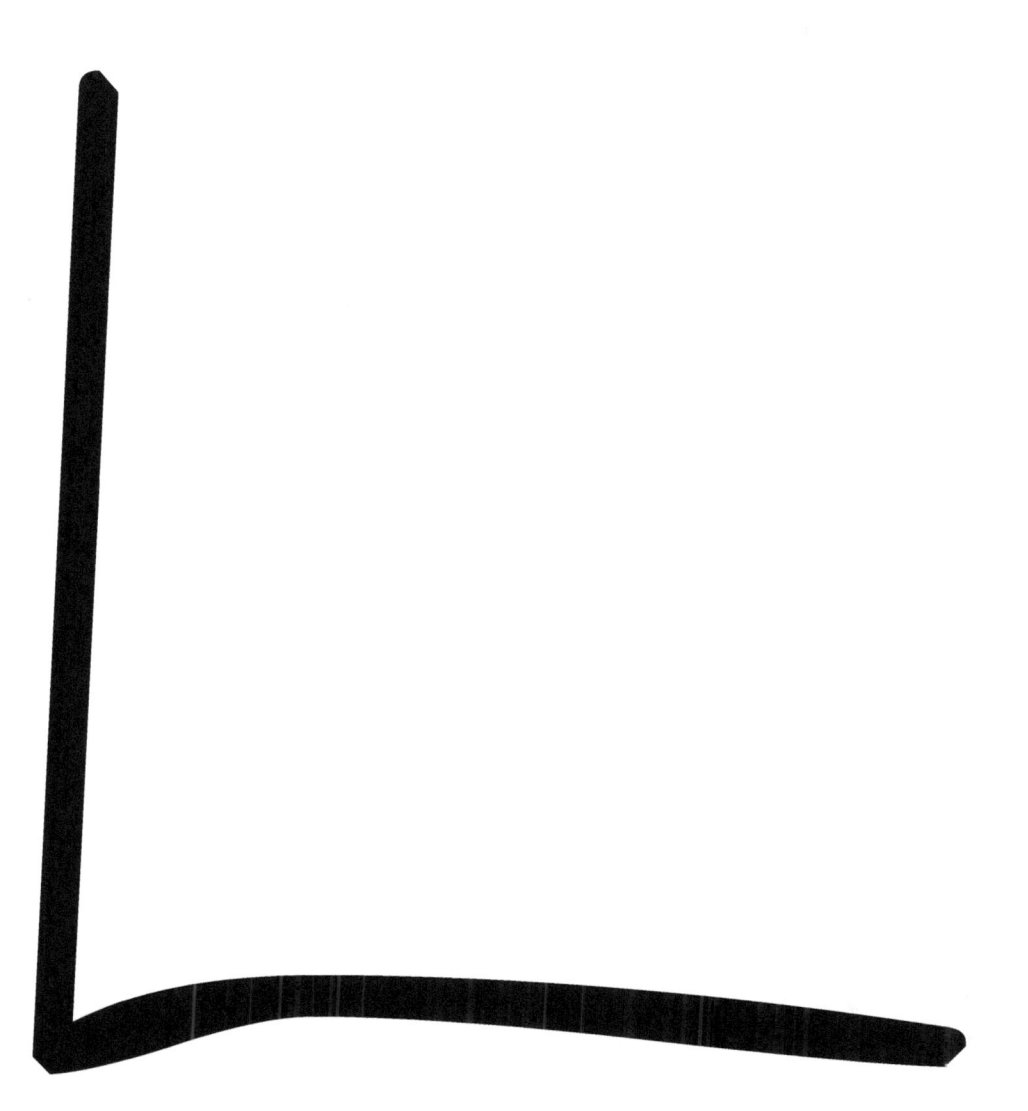

LABORATORY

In a dream to see a laboratory is a sign of grave peril ahead.

LABYRINTH

To try, in a dream, to find one's way through a maze or labyrinth is a waning of great worries and difficulties.

LACES

He spends his money too quickly or too freely who dreams of laces.

LADDER

To climb a ladder in your dream means success obtained by dangerous methods; to see yourself descending a ladder is a sign of total ruin and bankruptcy.

LAKE

The limpid waters of a lake, seen in a dream, speak of perfect friendship; while if the lake is either muddy or agitated, there is some quarrelling soon to worry you.

LAMP

A lighted lamp, seen in a dream, means extreme conceit; extinguished, it foretells the death of the dreamer.

LAMP-POST

There is success in store for one who sees a lighted lamp-post in a dream.

LANCE

Quarrelling will soon greatly annoy one who dreams of lances.

LANCET

Who dreams of a surgeon's lanecet will soon be overjoyed with goods news.

LANDAU

The carriage called a landau, when ever seen in a dream, is a threat of illness and money losses.

LANTERN

There is success in store for one who sees a lantern in his dream.

LARKS

To dream of larks (the birdies are here meant), is a sign of excellent luck; but if they are roasted, great troubles are about to break over your head.

LAUDANUM

Misfortune is in store for you if you dream of drinking or simply looking at a large dose of laudanum.

LAUGHING

If you laugh or hear any one laughing, in your dream, you may expect worries and losses.

LAUNDERING

You will be someone's slave for a long time yet, if not to your dying day, if you dream of laundry-work done either by you or by others.

LAUREL

In all shapes, laurel is a highly favorable omen.

LAWNS

To gaze upon lawns and grass-plots, is a sign of good health; to run over them is a prognostic of worries.

LAW-SUIT

Whoever dreams of law-suit, will soon go through separation proceedings or a divorce-trial.

LAWYERS

Dreaming of lawyers bespeaks many quarrels, worries, losses of time and money, with but slight final satisfaction, if any.

LEAD

To see lead in a dream means inheritance coming.

LEAVES

To dream of leaves is an omen of severe illness.

LEECHES

Help will come to you in the nick of time, if you dream of leeches.

LEGS

In a dream, legs mean success and plenty of money; but wooden legs are ominous to a degree.

LENTILS

To dream of lentils means that one of your close relatives is to be branded a scoundrel.

LEOPARD

The dreamer who dreams of a leopard, is himself a bragger and a scamp.

LEPROSY

You will surely make your money by undesirable means if you dream of being afflicted with leprosy or of simply gazing upon a leper.

LETTER-CARRIER

News is due very soon if you dream of a postman or letter-carrier.

LETTER

If you dream you are receiving a letter, expect one very soon from a far-off country if you see yourself writing one, that is evidence that your imagination is fertile.

LETTUCE

There is illness and trouble ahead for one who dreams of lettuce.

LICE

When you destroy lice, in a dream, you have much luck ahead; but if they are of the red variety, you must expect great poverty.

LIGHTNING

Flashes of lightning crossing your dream threaten you with a love-quarrel.

LIMP

To see in a dream someone limping badly, or to gaze upon one's self thus afflicted, warns you of great troubles in your business.

LINEN

To dream of linen, white goods, etc., is a sign of riches coming.

LION

The roaring of the lion, heard in a dream, is an omen of death; to see one's self killing or taming a lion, is a promise of great success; to see one in a cage, means some new friendship coming to you as a blessing.

LIONESS

To dream of a lioness is an omen of peace.

LIQUOR

There is riches in prospect for one who dreams of liquor.

LIZARDS

There are pitfalls in the way of one who dreams of lizards.

LOBSTER

To dream of a live lobster means success; of a cooked one, joy.

LOCK

To dream of door-locks is a promise of security and quiet.

LOCOMOTIVE

You may expect many worries and an unpleasant journey forced upon you, (you dream of a railroad engine.

LOTO

In a dream, the game of loto means trouble and loss.

LOTTERY

There are nothing but losses and failure in store for one who dreams of lotteries

LOW-NECK DRESS

Worn by a pretty lady, a low-neck dress, seen in a dream, is an omen of marriage; if the lady is plain—or worse—very serious worries will be the dreamer's lot.

LYRE

In a dream, one who sees a lyre may expect a funeral.

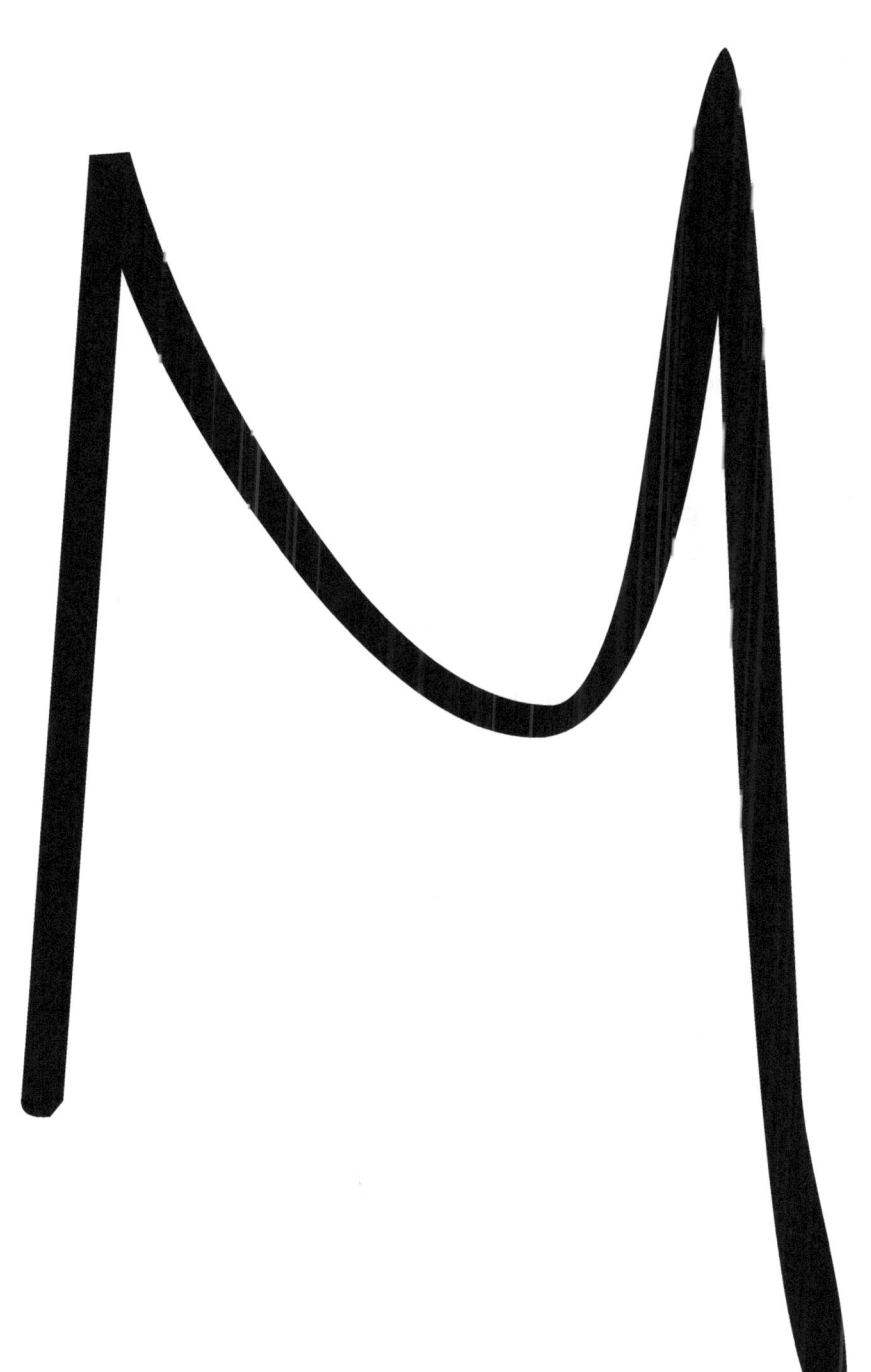

MACADAM

To dream of a macadamized road is a sign of safe investments and comfortable circumstances.

MACARONI

Whoever sees or tastes macaroni in his dream will soon be face to face with poverty.

MAGICIAN

There is warning of treachery at work against the dreamer who sees a magician or conjurer in his sleep.

MAGPIES

To see "one" magpie is a sign of bad luck; if you see "two" at the same time, the success of the enterprise you are engaged in will hang a long time in the balance, if you see "three" magpies, the worst luck awaits you. To counteract this bad influence hasten to touch iron.

MAIZE

In a dream, maize or corn is an omen of prosperity; but empty cornstalks mean poverty ahead.

MAN-OF-WAR

The sight of a war-vessel in a dream is assurance of a pleasurable voyage soon to be undertaken; but if the man-of-war is seen by you in a disabled condition, expect some great misfortune.

MANTILLA

There is deceit at work against one who dreams of a Spanish mantilla.

MAN

To dream of a man is a sign of unpleasant gossip; if he is very plain-looking, expect quarrel; if he is colored, you are threatened with trouble and money-losses.

MANURE

In a dream, the sight of manure, especially if you are soiled by it, is an omen of great financial luck.

MANUSCRIPT

To dream of some ancient manuscript, yellow with age, means that the dreamer will soon give evidence of inventive genius.

MARBLE

A block of marble seen in a dream means a coming inheritance.

MARMALADE

To dream of marmalade is a detestable prognostic.

MARMOT

Whoever dreams of a marmot will be affected with chronic laziness and indifference.

MARRIAGE

To dream of a marriage with a relative is an omen of danger: with a handsome person, there is joy in store; with a plain looking one, sorrow will be your lot.

MASQUERADING

To see one's self or another, in a mask and disguise, in a dream, is a sign of duplicity.

MATCHES

Sulphur matches, seen or smelled in a dream, are sign of quarrelling and deceiving from which the dreamer will greatly suffer.

MATTRESS

There is danger announced by a dream in which a mattress is in evidence.

MAUSOLEUM

Seen in a dream, a mausoleum or monumental tomb, means at the same time marriage, a birth and an inheritance, all due within a year.

MAY-BUGS

Agricultural failure, will be the lot of one who dreams of May bugs.

MEAT

To set yourself eating meat, in a dream, is a token of joy ahead.

MEDICINE

To see one's self swallowing some medicine is an omen of illness and worries.

MELON

No better omen of success than the dream of melons.

MENAGERIE

To dream of a menagerie be assured that you will be blessed with the gift of a sincere friendship.

MENDING

Clothes and stockings being mended in a dream, especially if the dreamer is doing the work, means an inheritance soon to come his way.

MERCHANDISE

To see, in a dream, merchandise piled about, means that you are being robbed at home.

MERCHANT

To dream that you meet a merchant of some importance is for you an omen of success in your favorite enterprise.

MESHES

To dream of any kind of mesh means losses and worries.

MESSAGE

To see one's self receiving a message in a dream is an omen of advancement in one's profession or trade.

MEOWING

If a cat is heard meowing at night, it means that the soul of a departed friend or relative is asking for prayers in its behalf.

MICE

To dream of a mouse, or mice, announces most serious troubles.

MIDWIFE

Expect much gossiping and a probable child-birth if you dream of a midwife.

MILL

To dream of a mill means a legacy coming to you very soon.

MILL-DAM

If you see a mill-dam, or the flood-gate or lock or sluice of a canal or river, in your dream, be assured that pain and torment are in store for you.

MINE

To dream of a mine in operation to a omen of danger.

MINUET

In a dream to take part in the old-time dance called the minuet is an omen of inheritance; just to see one danced foretells many worries.

MIRROR

In a dream, to gaze at your own face, in a mirror, is a token of love; but simply to see a mirror in your sleep, means treason.

MISTLETOE

To see or pluck a twig of mistletoe is an omen of excellent health.

MONEY

To dream that you are finding money is luck; that you are saving it, is a sign of sure loss; that you are counting it, means quarrelling; that you are simply gazing upon a lot of it, announces some one's treachery ; that you are swallowing some of it, is a token of fraud about to be committed by yourself.

MONEY-TROUBLES

To dream of money-troubles is a prognostic of complete success.

MONKEY

To dream of a monkey means that some enemy or cheat is about defrauding you of your property.

MONK

In a dream to see a monk means legacy in the near future.

MONSTERS

All kinds of monsters appearing, in a dream, are most unfortunate omens.

MOON

To dream of the moon throwing dear light, means love and purest affection in for you; a reddish moon is an omen of fame fortune; a clouded moon means the death of someone close to you; a full moon is a sign of great comfort and a new moon prognosticates a flirtation of importance.

MOON

When you see the moon surrounded by a clear circle, you may be sure that there will soon be a downpour.

MORGUE

To visit a morgue in your dream is a warning of death among your nearest friends.

MORNING

To see one's self in the early morning means positive success.

MOROCCO

There is success predicted by a dream wherein morocco plays a part.

MORTIFICATION

If you dream that gangrene or mortification is attacking you or someone else, it is a warning of death.

MOSAIC

To dream of mosaic or some inlaid piece of furniture or jewelry is an omen of catastrophe.

MOSQUITOES

Who dreams of mosquitoes will be the victim of envious hatred.

MOTH

A large moth persistently turning around your lamp at night foretells the coming of news.

MOTHER

To see one's mother in a dream is a sign of happiness and peace; to give her blows means disaster; to kill her foretells the dreamer's death.

MOUNTAIN

To dream of a very high mountain means great luck; if it is covered, your success will be still greater.

MOURNING

To see yourself dressed in deep mourning, in a dream, means a very merry time in the immediate future.

MOUTH

A small mouth seen in a dream, announces a flirtation; if it is wide, you will be blessed with a faithful friendship; if it shows ill-kept a deep sorrow threatens you.

MOVING

To dream of furniture-moving change of home is a sign that you will soon be the victim of treacherous and thieving individuals.

MOWING

To see, in a dream, yourself or someone else mowing is an assurance of great comfort.

MUD

Just to dream of mud is a sign of peaceful future; to wade through it is a promise of extraordinary success.

MUFF

He who dreams of a muff is filled with conceit.

MULE

You are sure to lose your court if you dream of a mule.

MUMMY

It is a sign of chronic and even serious illness to gaze upon a mummy in a dream.

MURDERERS

If you dream of murderers there is much fatigue in store for you; if you dream they are killing you, gravest danger ahead.

MUSHROOMS

To see, to gather, or to eat mushrooms in a dream is a sure sign of quarrelling and often of a broken engagement.

MUSIC

In a dream, to make music or simply to hear some is a promise of money and bliss in the near future.

MUSICAL INSTRUMENTS

There is a marriage and many gay hours in store for one who dreams of musical instruments.

MUSICAL SCALES

If you hear, in your dream, musical scales sung or played, there is luck ahead for you.

MUSSELS

To see or to eat mussels in dream is evidence of the dreamer's depravity.

MUSTACHES

Many quarrels and insults torment one who dreams of mustaches.

MUSTARD

In a dream, to see mustard is an omen of quarrelling.

MYRTLE

There is a marriage for yon shortly after you have dreamed of myrtle.

MYSTERIES

To dream of mysteries and if you try in vain to solve them, means that flatteries will soon be at work trying to cheat you.

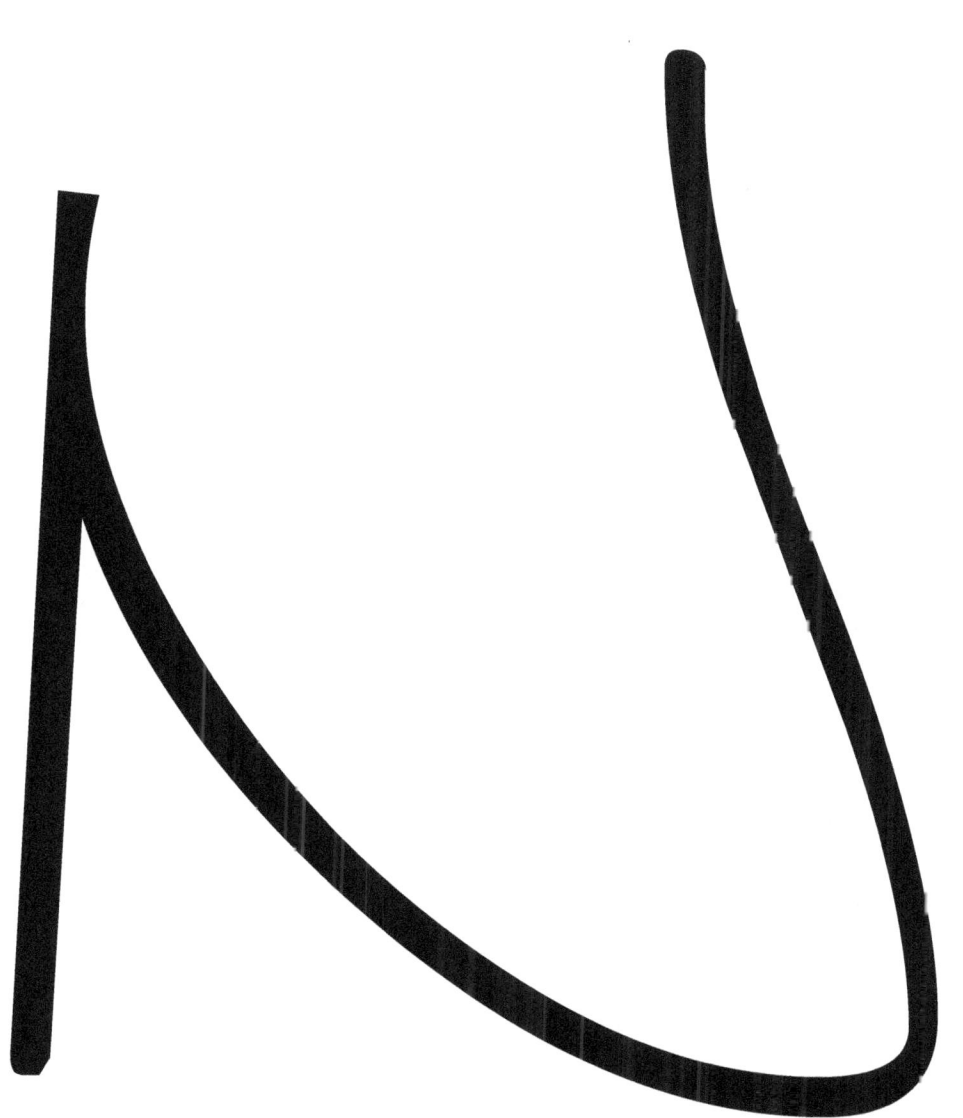

NAILS

To dream of nails is a threat of worries; if they are made of wood (in reality "pegs" and not "nails") your morals are very bad.

NAKEDNESS

To dream of someone entirely naked is a sure sign of treachery at work to ruin yon; if you see yourself running about naked or nearly so, insanity is threatening you; if you see yourself leaving a room suddenly on discovering your state of nudity, you may be assured that yon will soon suffer a mortal affront.

NAPE

To cut the nape of one's neck or to see it done before you in a dream means great success ahead.

NEAR-SIGHTEDNESS

To dream that you are near-sighted is a promise of long life.

NEEDLESS

Love-sorrows are the share of anyone who dreams of needles.

NEIGHBORS

To dream of neighbors of either sex means gossip of a harmful kind.

NEST

There is happiness and plenty of money in a dream wherein a bird-nest appears.

NETS

Either hunting or fishing nets appearing in a dream mean many troubles and money losses.

NETTLES

In a dream nettles always mean worries and losses.

NEWSPAPERS

If you dream of newspapers you are about to be made aware of some treason concocted at your expense.

NIGHTINGALE

If you hear or simply see a nightingale in a dream, it is a promise of fidelity and peace.

NIGHT

To dream of darkness or night is an omen of sadness.

NOODLES

That German dish called "noodles," appearing in a dream, is an omen of dire poverty.

NOSE

To dream of a nose of average sin means that you will soon be penniless; if it is very thick, good luck to you; very long, a numerous family; crooked, a woman is about to deceive you; to see yourself noseless, means that your moral will go from bad to worse.

NUMBNESS

To dream that yon are entirely or partially benumbed is a sign of poor sleep, of chronic illness and of feminine deceit.

NUNS

There is a legacy coming very soon to one who dreams of nuns.

NURSE

A private or hospital nurse appearing in your dream, gives you promise of a long spell of fine health.

NUTS

To see nuts or hazelnuts in a dream means many cares and narrow circumstances.

OBELISK

To see in a dream an obelisk is a sign of trouble and grief.

OCCULTIST

In dream that you visit an occultist means that you will foil in time a plot against you.

OIL

The cream of oil means success, satisfaction, fine crops.

OLIVES

In a dream olive trees or olives are decidedly lucky omens.

OMNIBUS

There is anxiety and heavy loss in store for one who sees an omnibus in his dream.

ONE-ARMED

To dream of yourself, or someone else, having but one arm is an omen of many worries.

ONIONS

Cooked onions, in a dream, security; raw onions foretell quarrels.

ORANGES

Much satisfaction will be the one who sees or eats oranges in a dream.

ORANGUTAN

Whoever dreams of the big monkey called an "orangutan" will surely be the victim of a fraud.

ORATOR

To hear an orator in your dream means that you will soon be cheated unmercifully.

ORCHESTRA

To listen to a band or orchestra in a dream is a most favorable omen.

ORGAN

To play the organ or to hear it played is a lucky prognostic; if it is a church-organ it is an omen of death.

OSTRICH

To dream of an ostrich is a token of painful disappointment.

OWL

Sadness and even death will soon come to one who dreams of an owl.

OYSTER-SHELLS

In a dream, mean losses and worries.

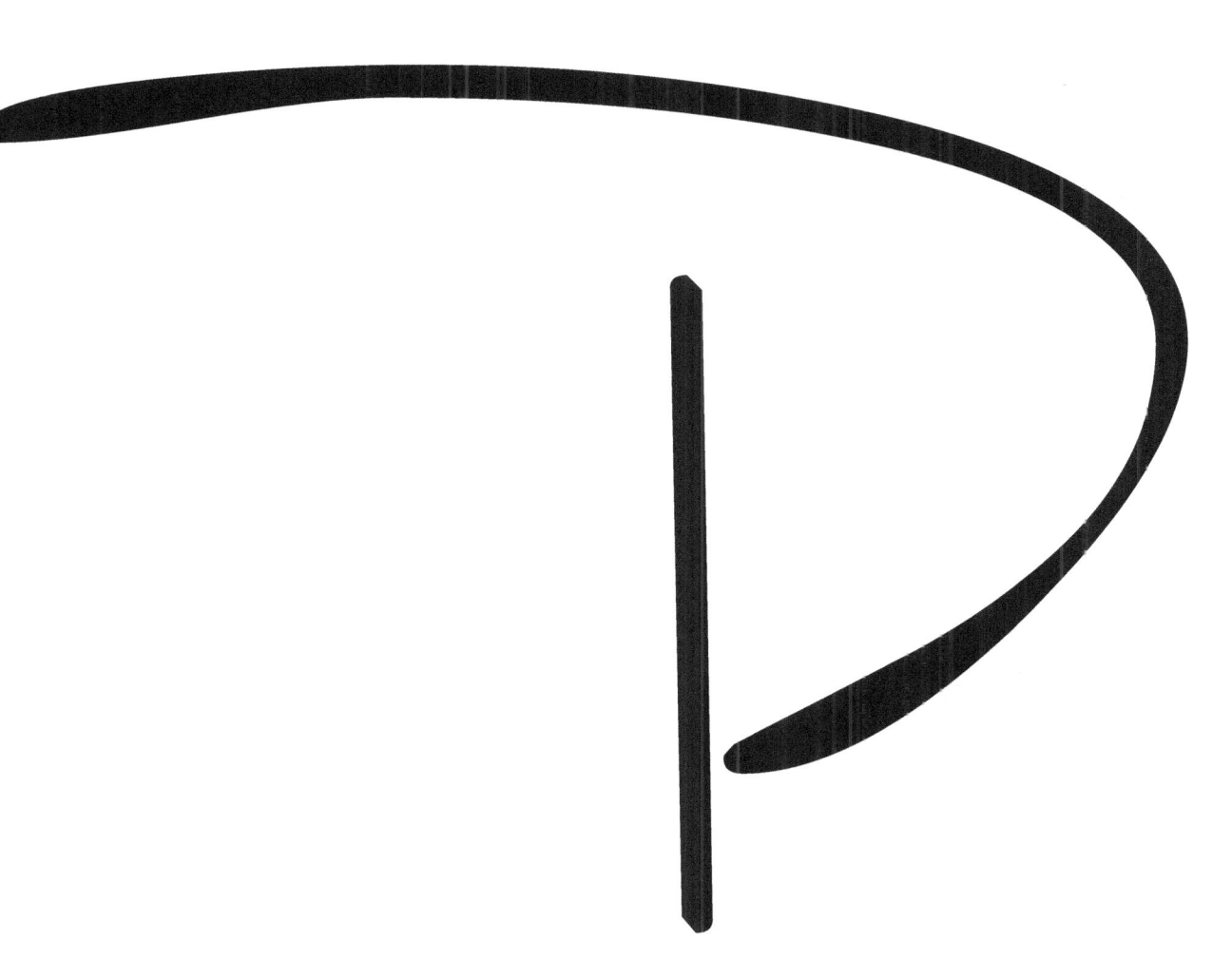

PADDED-CELL

Only sadness and deepest despondency can result from a dream wherein you see yourself in an insane asylum's padded-cell.

PADLOCK

To dream of a padlock means that all the precautions you are so carefully taking will be of no avail.

PAGODA

The Chinese building, known as a "pagoda," seen in a dream, promises an inheritance.

PAIN

If you feel physical pain, in a dream, your luck will be growing better every day.

PAINT

To dream of receiving paint on one's hands and clothes means dishonor and ruin in the near future; if you see yourself daubing someone else with paint, you have pleasant times ahead.

PAINTER'S BRUSHES

There is an omen of success in painter's brushes when seen in a dream.

PALACE

Many troubles are in store for him who dreams of a palace.

PALM-TREE

To dream of a palm-tree is a most favorable omen.

PANORAMA

Seen in a dream, a panorama means many serious troubles in the near future.

PANTHER

There is hatred and duplicity and work against one who sees a panther in his dream; if he sees himself killing it, he will surely triumph over his treacherous enemies.

PANTOMIME

To witness, in a dream, an old-fashioned pantomime is to be promised much success and great profits.

PAPER

White paper, in a dream, means news on the way; colored paper foretells treachery at work.

PARADISE

To dream of paradise is an omen of death.

PARK

To see or visit a park, in a dream, means financial advancement and happiness; but if the park is poorly kept, there are great losses ahead.

PARLIAMENT

To dream of the British Parliament, American Congress, French House of Deputies or German Reichstag is a warning that there is treachery on foot to ruin you.

PARRICIDE

To dream that you are committing, or witnessing, a parricide, is an omen of terrible anxieties and sorrow; probably death.

PARROT

In a dream, a parrot means that wicked people are gossiping at your expense.

PASSING-BELL

To hear the knell or passing-bell in a dream, is an omen of death for the dreamer.

PASTRY

There are worries in store for one who dreams of pastry or pastry-cook.

PATENT-MEDICINE

To dream of some "cure-all" patent-medicine is a lucky omen.

PAWNSHOP

To dream of a pawnshop is a warning that you will soon be deserted, and in want.

PEACHES

Many joys are promised to one who dreams of peaches.

PEACOCK

The dreamer who sees a peacock in his sleep is most certainly conceited to an extreme degree.

PEARLS

Appearing in a dream pearls foretell of bad times and straightened circumstances.

PEARS

To dream that you ere gathering pearls is a promise of pleasure; that you are eating pears is an omen of death.

PEAS

To see green peas is a sign of health: but if they are already cooked, illness is very near.

PEBBLES

Sorrows and worries follow the sight of pebbles in a dream.

PENALTIES

All penalties, especially fines, which you dream of, mean that you are going to be extraordinarily successful.

PERFUMES

If you smell perfumes in your dream you will meet with the greatest success in your enterprises.

PERSIAN CAT

You will soon be fobbed if you see a Persian cat (one with long hair and blue eyes) in your dream.

PEST

Misfortune and poverty threaten one who dreams of a pest or plague.

PHEASANTS

To dream of pheasants is favorable; to see yourself shooting pheasants, great danger ahead.

PHYSICIAN

It is a highly favorable prognostic to dream of a physician.

PICTURES

There are many worries in store for one who dreams he is gazing at pictures

PIEBALD ANIMAL

When you meet a piebald horse or cow, hasten to make a wish; it will be granted you.

PIG

To dream of a pig is most tacky as to all money matters.

PIMPERNEL

When the pimpernel closes its flowers, rain is imminent.

PIMPLES

In a dream, all kinds of pimples or pustules, are interpreted as announcing excellent fortune ahead.

PINCERS

To see or hold pincers or nippers is an omen of cruel anxieties.

PINEAPPLES

To dream of pineapples means profits coming; but if you eat some in your dream, your wife (or husband) is about to deceive you.

PINS

To pick up and keep a stray pin is the most serious sign of good luck.

PIPE

To see or smoke a pipe in a dream, is a promise of delightful quiet.

PIPING

There is luck in store for whoever dreams of pipes or underground conduits.

PLASTER

Sorrow and suffering are the meaning of plaster seen in a dream.

PLATE

To dream that you are purchasing silverware is an assurance of persistent poverty; you see such goods but do not buy them, this announces to you a family gathering soon to taking place.

PLOWING

To see plowing done, or yourself, in a dream, handling a plow, is an omen of joy and plenty.

PLOWS

There is some serious misfortune close at hand when you dream of a plow.

PLUMS

In a dream, fresh plums are an excellent prognostic; dried plums or prunes foretell serious worries.

POISON

Grave misfortune will assail one who dreams of poison.

POLE-CAT

If you see a pole-cat in your dream, be assured that someone is plotting your undoing.

POLICEMAN

If a "Bobby" or "Cop" or "gendarme" appears in your dream, dishonor and disaster will be waiting for you when you awake.

POLISHING

In your dream, if you do, or see anyone doing, some active polishing, you may depend that there is lots of unpleasant quarrelling in store for you in the near future,

POLITICIANS

To dream of politicians prognosticates endless and fruitless discussions.

POOL

To gaze into a clear pool, in a dream, gives promise of sincere friendship; if the water muddy, quarrels are in sight; if dead fish float on the surface, dire poverty will soon stare you in the face.

POP

To dream of pop announces a birth soon to happen.

POPE

A vision of the pope in your dream means your death within a short space of time.

POPLARS

To dream of poplars, if they are green with leaves, is a token of hope; if they are leafless or shattered, only cares are in store for you; if you see yourself climbing a poplar tree, you may consider luck to be with you.

PORK AND SAUSAGE

The sundry articles of food made from hog's meat, etc., whenever they appear in a dream are prognostics of a remarkable run of luck.

PORRINGER

To dream of any kind of porringer or platter such as the sailors and soldiers use at meals is a token of great riches coming.

PORTRAIT

In dream, a portrait means bliss for the one whose face it represents; should you destroy a portrait in a dream, it is an omen of death.

PREACHING

In your dream, to be listening to a sermon means that the dreamer is good and kind at heart.

PRECIPICE

In a dream to fall into a precipice or simply to gaze into one, is a warning of treachery.

PRESENT

Receiving a present in your dream is a token of many worries; if it comes from a man, hatred will be the consequence; from a maiden, an engagement will be broken; from a married woman great danger ahead in the very near future.

PRIEST

To meet a priest in his black cassock is a very unfavorable omen. Should he touch you slightly, as he passes by, expect death to visit you very soon.

PRINTING-OFFICE

Many troubles are in store for him who dreams of a printing office.

PRISON

To dream that you are in prison is an omen of excellent luck; to see yourself escaping means temporary success.

PROCESSION

To witness, in a dream, the passing of a procession is a omen of heavy losses.

PROPERTY

Valuable property received as a gift, in a dream, means marriage with a person whose personal appearance and future will be on a par with the value of the property thus received. Thus important real estate presented to you in a dream is the prognostic of the happiest and most brilliant of marriages.

PUDDLE

It is very unlucky to dream of a water or mud puddle.

PULPIT

To dream that yon are standing in a pulpit denotes extravagant vanity; should you hear yourself preaching from the pulpit, many sorrows are in store for you.

PURCHASES

If you dream of making many purchases, there is a fortune on its way to your pockets.

PURSE

To see a purse in your dream means temporary prosperity, if it is empty, durable success; if it is full to overflowing, a token of mean habits and laziness; if you dream you are finding a purse, bankruptcy is imminent; if it is black, there are hopes for you; if it is blue, happiness is coming.

PYRAMIDS

A vision of pyramids in a dream is a most brilliant prognostic of success.

QUADRILLE

There is an inheritance in the near future if you witness yourself dancing a quadrille; but if you are only a spectator expect nothing but disappointment.

QUAIL

If you see a live quail in your dream it is a promise of good times; a dead one is a sign of much sadness.

QUARANTINE

Dreaming of quarantine lazaretto is a sign of wretched poverty.

QUARRELLING

To dream of your ling means reconciliation and friendship

QUARREL

To hear, in a dream, a quarrel taking place is the token of coming home trouble.

QUAYS

If you see a quay or embankment, in a dream, there is peace and comfort in store for you.

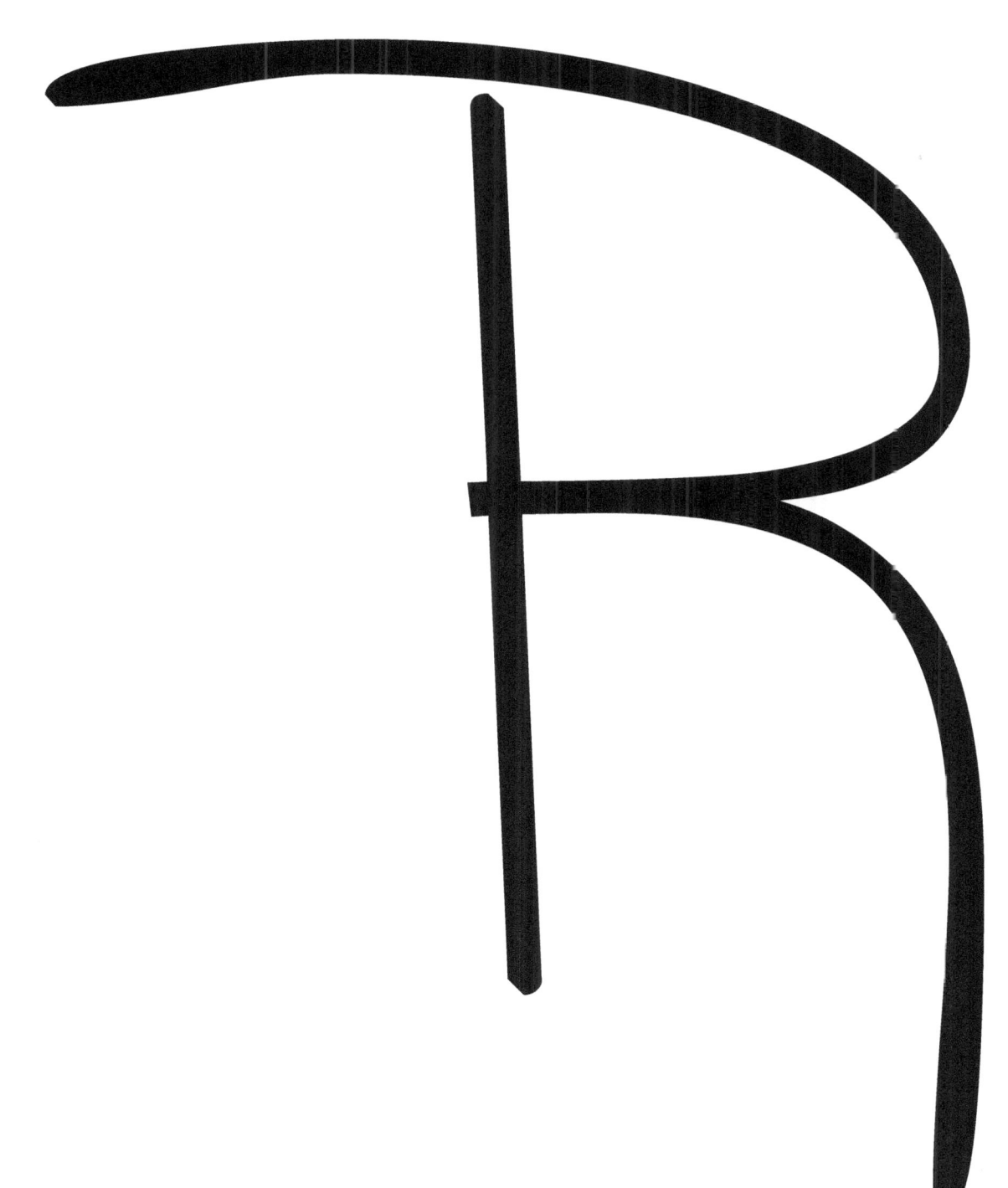

RABBIT

To dream of a white rabbit means success in spite of the dreamer's timidity; if it is black, worries will assail you.

RACKET

To play with a racket, or simply see one, in a dream, is a most lucky omen.

RADISHES

Whoever dreams of radishes is rare to have a large family.

RAFT

To see a raft in a dream is a sign of news coming.

RAGS

In a dream to see yourself or others in rags, is an omen of many "close shaves" and "hard pulls" ending in prosperity.

RAILING

To dream of a railing or grating announces great troubles and even imprisonment.

RAILROAD-CAR

Travel and unpleasantness of some kind are in store for one who merely dreamt of railroad-cars or trains.

RAILROAD

To see one's self on a railroad train in a dream is a sure omen of the dreamer being called upon to make a very long journey.

RAINBOW

In a dream a rainbow is a pit of temporary estrangement, sometimes even to the breaking of an engagement.

RAIN

To see rain falling is a promise of inheritance for the dreamer, but if it is a rainstorm, he may expect serious worries.

RAM'S-HORNS

To dream of ram's horns is threat of great dishonor coming.

RATS

Treachery is at work ruining you, when you dream of rats.

RAZOR

No luck is in store for whoever dreams of a razor.

READING

In a dream, to see yourself reading some serious work means that you will soon be advanced in your profession; if the book read is a novel, you will enjoy fleeting satisfaction.

REINDEER

There is much luck for one who sees a reindeer in a dream.

REPTILE

There is much luck in store for one who kills a snake by accident when mowing wheat or grass.

REPTILES

All kinds of reptiles appearing in a dream warn you that you are being cheated or soon will be.

RIBBONS

In a dream to see ribbons means that the dreamer is more or less of a spendthrift.

RICE

If you see yourself, in a dream, eating rice, expect great prosperity; but if you push it aside disdainfully, nothing but want is in store for you.

RICH PEOPLE

In a dream, to associate with rich people is a promise of fortune and position coming to you very soon.

RICHES

To dream that you are very rich is a threat of great poverty.

RINGS

There is promise of high honors for one who dreams he is wearing a heavy gold ring. Should you dream that a ring is given to you, you may feel perfectly safe; if you are the giver, only troubles and losses are in store for you.

RIVER

A clear, large river, in your dream, prophecies security; if the water is muddy, there are worries and losses ahead.

ROAD

To see one's self on a high-road or causeway is a sign of many troubles.

ROAST

Comfort is meant by a dream of roast, or roasting-pan.

ROCKS

In a dream, to see rocks means worries; to see one's self climbing rocks is an omen of final success.

ROOF

Great luck will come to one who sees a roof in his dream.

ROOSTER

Seen in a dream, a rooster means power and proud distinction to be bestowed upon the dreamer.

ROOTS

In a dream, just to see roots of plants or trees means poverty coming. To eat roots is an omen of feminine treachery.

ROPE

To dream of any kind of rope (except one for hanging a man) is a threat of money troubles.

ROSES

There is general good fortune and happiness in the fact of seeing roses in a dream; yellow roses, however, signify great trouble ahead.

ROUGE

To dream of rouge or facial make-up, signifies that treason is at work against you.

ROW-BOAT

If you dream of a row-boat, good news is to reach you very soon; if you see the boat upset, your health will be greatly disturbed.

RUINS

To gaze upon a ruined building in a dream is a most fortunate omen.

RUNNING

To see, in a dream, running, is a threat of bad news and much order; if you see game running away, it is a sign of financial loss; if you see yourself running, there is much anxiety in store for you; should you be naked besides, insanity is threatening you; if in your dream you are running away in a great fright, you will soon take to flight in reality.

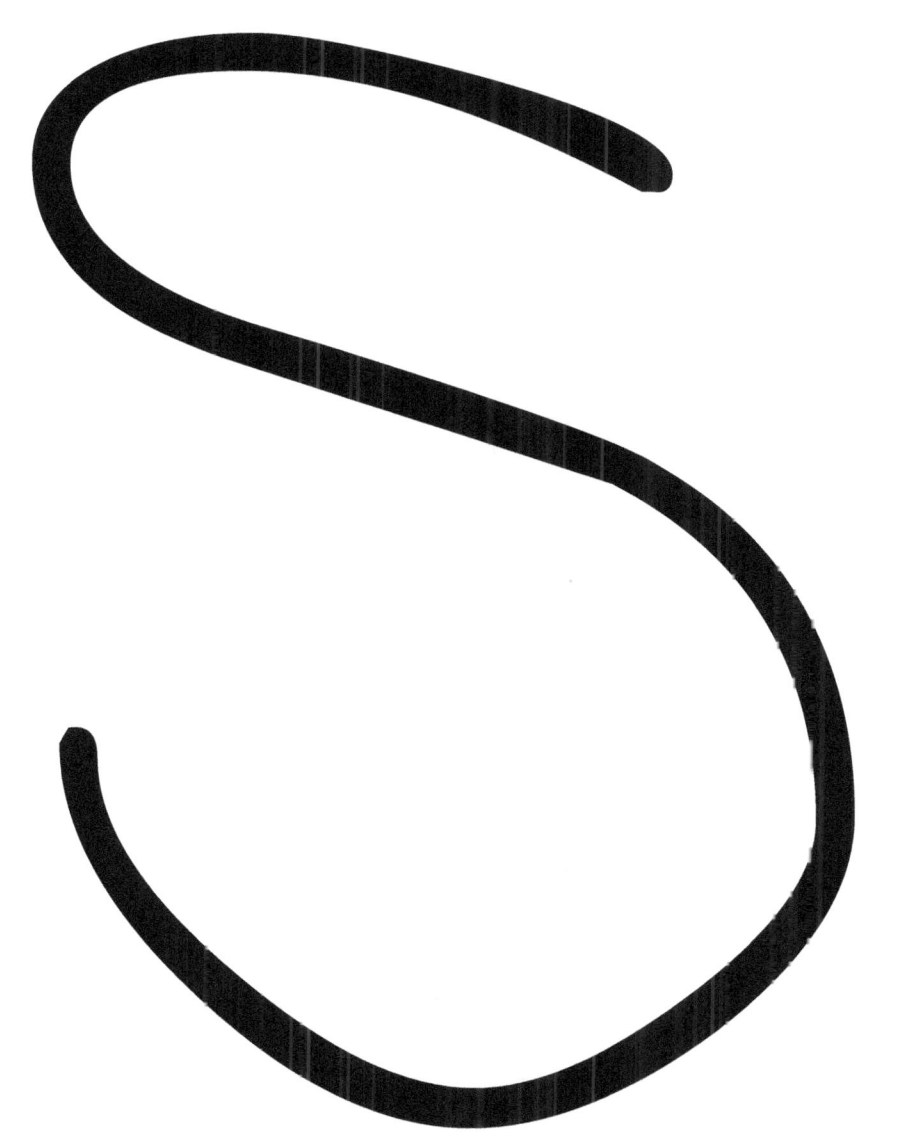

SAFE

An iron or steel safe or strong box appearing in a dream means money coming, but not to be in your possession very long.

SAILORS

There is poverty and unpleasant voyages in store for one who dreams of sailors.

SALAD

A maiden who prepares a salad of greens risks to have to wait, before she marries, as many years as she will allow leaves of salad to drop out of the salad-bowl.

SALAD

To eat, or simply to see, salad in a dream, is a threat of financial difficulties.

SALMON

In a dream, to eat salmon is omen of separation.

SALT

Many worries will be the lot of one who dreams of salt.

SCAFFOLD

The vision of a scaffold, in a dream, is a most favorable omen of triumphant success.

SCAFFOLDING

There is much disappointment and no little failure to expect if you dream of scaffolding surrounding a building.

SCISSORS

In a dream, scissors are always a sign of quarrelling and of some grave illness coining.

SCRATCHES

If you dream of scratches, and gossip will play havoc with your reputation.

SCREECH-OWL

Seen in a dream, a screech-owl announces a coming death in the family.

SEA

Just to dream of the sea signifies you will soon undertake a journey; if the sea it placid, you will meet with business reverses; if it is much agitated, your financial ruin will be completed very soon.

SEAL

When a seal appears in your dream, you are sure to marry for love.

SENTRY

Seen in a dream, a sentry means peace and quiet.

SENTRY-BOX

You may feel safe and secure after having dreamed of a sentry box.

SERENADE

To dream that someone is serenading you is a most lucky sign.

SERVANTS

To dream of servants always means idle gossip and quarrelling.

SEWING OMEN

When sewing in a group with other girls, if you sew by accident the stuff you handle with that which one of your neighbors is sewing on, the latter will soon marry; if you have the same accident with two different pieces in your own lap, you will soon be a bride.

SHANTY

A half dilapidated cottage or shanty in your dream is a token of great prosperity coming.

SHARK

The appearance of sharks in a dream is a warning of danger, disease and death.

SHE-APE

Expect deceit and fraud to hurt you if you dream of a female monkey.

SHEAVES

To dream of sheaves means plenty of money.

SHEEP

Much luck and large profits will be the lot of one who dreams of sheep.

SHE-GOATS

To dream of white Nanny-goats, is a sign of happiness; if they are black, illness is threatened.

SHEPHERD

There is a threat of mourning in the appearance of a shepherd in one's dream.

SHIP

There is a journey, and a successful one soon to be undertaken by one who dreams of a ship. If it is in danger, great riches will come to you; if sinks, a terrible peril awaits you.

SHOE-BLACKING

If you see your shoes being blackened in your dream, death or ruin is about to stare you in the face.

SHOES

To dream of shoes is a threat of scandal ending in dishonor; if the shoes are worn, there's a long journey in prospect for you.

SHOT-GUN

Any kind of shot gun or rifle in a dream announces great wretchedness in a short time.

SHOULDERS

If broad and strong, shoulders appearing in a dream are a most lucky omen; if thin and low, they prognosticate troubles galore.

SHROUD

A shroud appearing in a dream, is a promise of inheritance.

SICK-HEADACHE

To suffer from sick-headache in a dream, is an omen of death in the family.

SILK CAP

In a dream, to see a silk cap is a lucky omen.

SILK

Whoever dreams of silk will be blessed lucky and large profits.

SILK-SKEIN

To dream of a skein of silk means great success and large profits.

SILK-WORMS

Much success is in store for one who dreams of silk-worms.

SILVERWARE

To dream that you own valuable silverware is a threat of money-losses, but your affairs will improve materially if you see yourself disposing of silverware.

SINGING

If you dream that you hear singing in a church, distress and anxiety will be your lot, the singing of birds means conjugal infidelity. Should you yourself sing in your dream, the deepest sorrow, even to the despairing point, will be in store for you.

SKATE

In a dream, to eat or simply to see that ugly, but excellent fish, called skate, is an excellent prognostic.

SKATING

To dream of skating with others, means difficulties ahead.

SKELETON

To dream of a skeleton is an omen of death.

SKY

To see one's self gating at the sky, in a dream, is a lucky prognostic; if the sky is blue, a fortune is coming to the dreamer; if it is red, there is great danger ahead. To feel yourself rising, or coming down, through the air, means general failure in all your plans.

SLEEP

To dream that you are asleep means that your confidence is based on foolish illusions.

SLEIGH-BELLS

Home-quarrels are foretold by the sight or sound of sleigh-bells in one's dream.

SLIDING

To see in a dream, one's self or some one else, sliding, is a warning of trouble ahead.

SLING

A slung-shot or sting, to dream, means troubles, insults and slanderous attacks in store for the dreamer.

SLIPPERS

To see a pair of slippers in your dream is a promise of peace and quiet.

SMOKE

Vain and fruitless ambition will be the lot of one who sees smoke in his dream.

SNAILS

The dreamer has immoral habits who sees snails in his sleep.

SNAKES

To dream of serpents is a sure sign that treachery is at work against you. If you are not ill, you will become so very soon; if you are already ill, you will surely be worse.

SNOUT

A pig's snout, seen in a dream, is an excellent omen.

SNOW-FLAKES

There is a most favorable omen in the apparition of falling snow-flake.

SNOW

To dream that you see snow means a plentiful harvest; that you are washing your face with snow, is a promise of great relief; that you are eating some, is a prognostic of a journey soon to be undertaken.

SOAP

There is success in store for whoever dreams of soap.

SOCIETY-MANNERS

If, in a dream, you see yourself or others performing all sorts of exaggerated and affected society antics, there is some grave danger ahead.

SOFT MUD

To see one's self wading through soft mud is a prognostic of much money coming very soon.

SOLDIERS

To dream of soldiers is either a warning of danger or the announcement of good news very soon to reach you.

SOLES

In a dream to eat of die fish called a sole, is an omen of poverty.

SON

To dream that you have a son, it a sign of a birth soon due.

SOOT

If soot drops on you, in a dream, expect large profits within a short time.

SOUP

To eat soup, or simply to see some, is a promise of riches coming.

SPARROW

In a dream, one sparrow is profits coming; many sparrows prognosticate journey soon to take place.

SPECTACLES

Old fashioned spectacles eye-glasses, in a dream, tell you that you are blind and silly in your waking hours.

SPECTRE

White-robed spectres seen in a dream threaten you with disaster due to a trusted friend's treachery; black-robed spectre the harbingers of a great joy.

SPEECHES

To hear speeches in a dream result in bringing about many troubles.

SPIDER

To see one in your dream is, at night, a token of hopeful success; in the morning, a sign of troubles ahead; if in your dream you are killing it, great joy is coming: that you are eating it, a luckier sign still, but that dream is very rare.

SPINDLE

There is trouble, plotting, and disappointment for one who sees a spindle in his dream.

SPINNING

To see in a dream, yourself or someone else, spinning is a threat of many serious worries.

SPONGES

The miserly disposition of the dreamer is revealed to him, when he sees sponges in his sleep.

SPOOLS OF THREAD

Betrayal, anguish, and ruin will be forthcoming if you dream of spools of thread.

SPOTS

If you dream of spots or stains, it tells you that you are yourself a specimen of a very lazy, worthless individual.

SPURS

There is the announcement of a journey in a dream wherein spurs play a part.

SQUALL

To witness a squall of wind in a dream announces a quarrel among close relatives.

SQUIRREL

To dream of a squirrel signifies that someone who robbed you is about to be caught and punished.

STABLE

A person you love is coming very soon to see you, after you see a stable in a dream.

STAGE-COACH

Seen in a dream, a coach is a prognostic of diseases and financial loss.

STAIR-BANNISTERS

To gaze in a dream upon stair-bannisters and to let the hand glide over them is a favorable omen; but if you let go of them, you may expect serious losses.

STAIRS

To see a staircase in your dream means profits coming; to fall down stairs is an omen of grief.

STARS

To dream of stars means complete bliss; but if they do not shine, sorrow is forthcoming; while a shooting star, in a dream, prophecies some near relative's death.

STATUES

In a dream, to see statues is a threat of coming sorrows.

STEEL

Dreaming of steel means success and promotions; but if the steel be burning hot, great worries are coming.

STEEPLE

To see a church-steeple in a dream, means great trouble due to a friend; if it is a ruined steeple you gaze upon, a terrible catastrophe is to overcome you very soon.

STILTS

Thwarted, disappointed ambition always follows a dream in which stilts are seen.

STOCKINGS

Cotton-stockings are, in dream, a sign of inheritance; silk-stockings, a promise of great riches, but not by inheritance.

STONE-MASONS

Whoever dreams of stone-masons at work may expect a birth in the family.

STONES

In a dream, stones are always to be interpreted as difficulties placed in your path.

STORE

To dream of a store means success.

STORKS

To dream of flying storks is an omen of enmity at work against you; if the season is winter, a terrible storm is brewing; but if they fly in pairs, a marriage will soon take place and be blessed with many children.

STORMING A FORT

It is an omen of quarrelling, when you see yourself, in a dream, storming a fortress; if you "storm" only a window, you are threatened with a woman's treachery.

STORMS

There is danger ahead for dreaming of a storm.

STOUT PERSON

If you dream of a very stout person, your success will be great and immediate.

STOVE

Quiet comfort and good news, are to be expected after you have seen a stove in your dreams.

STRAW

To dream of bundles of straw is a promise of plenty; but if it's in a heap, want will soon assail you. Burning straw carried about in a public place is an omen of great joy.

STRAWBERRIES

Riches are in store for you if you dream of strawberries.

STREET

If you see yourself in a dream, walking aimlessly about in a city street, many troubles await you in your own home.

STREET-POSTERS

To dream that you are reading posters in the street is an omen of infamous notoriety; if you see yourself tearing them down the deepest grief will soon be your lot; finally, if you are pasting them yourself on the walls, some terrible shame is in store for you. This is, altogether one of the worst dreams you may suffer from.

SUICIDE

To dream that you are committing suicide is a warning to you to change your conduct.

SUN

When the sun dazzles your eyes and, at the same time, your feet are walking in water or on wet ground, you may be assured that you will be married within a year.

SUNSHADE

To dream of a sunshade is foreboding of temporary sadness.

SUN

To gaze at the sun, in a dream, means happiness ahead.

SURGEON

Seen in a dream, a surgeon fore-tells joy and prosperity.

SWADDLING-CLOTHES

To dream of babies clothes is a promise of a most happy marriage.

SWALLOWS

There is the greatest happiness in sight for one who dreams of swallows.

SWAMP

You will soon be quarrelling if, in a dream, you see yourself in a swampy or marshy country.

SWANS

A vision of swans, in a dream, is a highly favorable omen.

SWEEPING

Who dreams that he is sweeping a room or a house may count upon prosperity; but if it is a cellar he is cleaning, evil happenings are sure to assail him.

SWEETHEART

To dream that you have a sweetheart, when you have none (at the time), is a foreboding of sorrow; to dream that you are deceiving the said sweetheart is a sign of bitter quarrelling in sight.

SWELLING

To see yourself swollen, in a dream, signifies that your intense vanity is about to be severely taken to task.

SWIMMING

In a dream, to see yourself, or someone else, swimming, means that some reconciliation is about to take place.

SWISS CHEESE

Many difficulties will obstruct your success, if you dream of Swiss cheese.

SWORD

To see a sword, in a dream, is an omen of disaster, or at least of quarrelling; to hold one firmly is a promise of good luck; to receive sword-wound means quarrelling; to inflict a wound with it to someone else, is a threat of a painful separation.

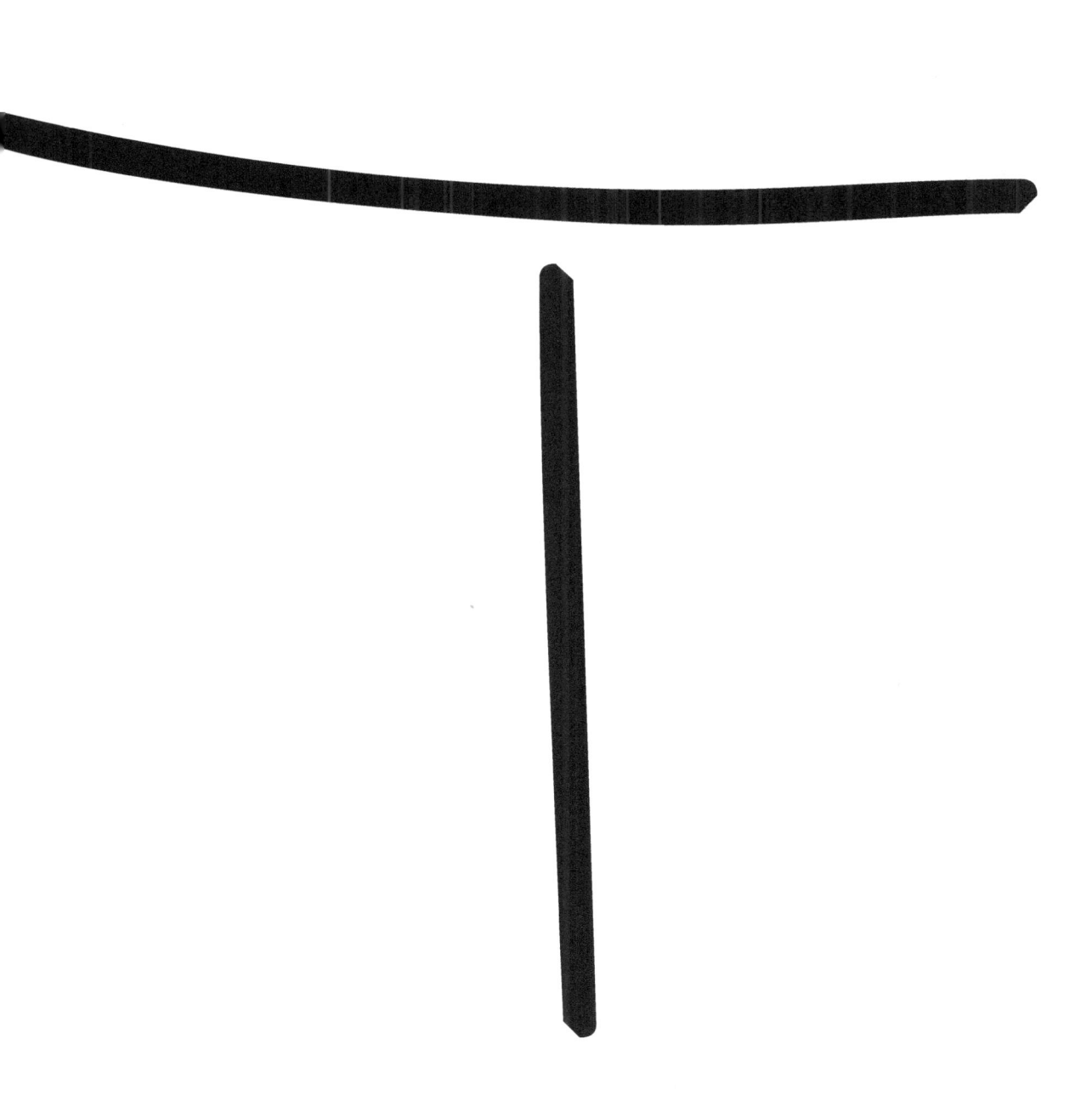

TABLE

To dream that you are setting a table for a meal, is a promise of abundance.

TAILOR

Appearing in a dream, a tailor signifies mendacity detrimental to your interests.

TEA

Many worries are in store for one who sees himself, in a dream, drinking tea.

TEARS

Success is assured to one who dreams of tears, or weeps in his sleep.

TEETH

To see teeth in a dream is a sign of great joy coming; it will last long if the teeth are very white; if they are very long, you will soon suffer wane; if they are decayed, there is mourning in the near future; if they fall off your gums of their own accord, death is imminent.

TELESCOPE

In a dream, a telescope means some act of silliness to be soon performed by the dreamer.

TEMPEST

Quarrelling and anguish will be the lot of one who dreams that he witnesses a tempest.

TEN-PINS

To play ten-pins, or just to gaze at them, in a dream is an omen of worries and loss.

TENT

There is quarrelling soon to occur when one dreams of a tent.

THEATRE

To dream that you are sitting in a theatre, means for you repose and satisfaction.

THERMOMETER

To dream of a thermometer means quarrelling.

THIMBLE

A thimble in a dream, means the loss of a situation.

THORNS

We always find in thorns dreamed of a sign of worries and often of loss of situation.

THREAD

To see thread in a dream is a threat of an intrigue against you; to break off a thread is an omen of poverty; to entangle a spool or skein of thread means that your affairs will soon be in the worst disorder; to unwind it is a sign of some indiscretion greatly harming you; finally, to dream of gold or silver thread is most unlucky.

THRONE

In the vision of a throne, in a dream, there is a threat of many cruel disappointments.

THUNDERBOLT

In a dream, the clashing and close striking of a thunderbolt announce great misfortunes and even death.

TIGER

There is hatred at work against you if you dream of a tiger; but if you see yourself killing it, you may expect great success.

TORCHES

In a dream, many lighted torches mean dazzling success.

TORNADO

To see or hear a tornado in a dream, signifies that some terrible danger is nigh.

TOWN-MARKET

Extreme poverty is in store for one who dreams of a town-market.

TOYS

Nothing but worries and disappointments are in store for one who dreams of toys and playthings.

TRADE

To dream of trade under any form is generally considered favorable; if it is of the silk trade, many pleasures are in store for you; the iron trade, many sorrows; the woolen trade, you will be robbed.

TRAVELING

To dream that you are traveling in a carriage is a promise of sudden fortune coming to you as a gift; if you are a-foot, you can expect pretty hard work in prospect; if you have a traveling companion, people are talking about you ; if you see yourself trudging along with a sword at your side, yon are to marry very soon.

TURKISH PIPE

Whoever dreams that he is smoking or simply looking at someone else smoking a Turkish pipe, has much peace in store for him.

TURKISH SLIPPERS

Seen in a dream, Turkish slippers, if new, mean success after very hard and laborious struggles; if worn out, you are about to undertake a small journey.

TURTLE

If you see a turtle in a dream, beware of some secret enemy; if you see yourself eating turtle flesh, expect success after a pretty hard struggle.

TWIN-FRUITS

There is good luck in store for one who meets with twin-fruits, that is, a fruit with two stones instead of one.

TYPHUS OR TYPHOID

A dream in which typhus or typhoid fever acts a part is a threat of terrible illness and even death.

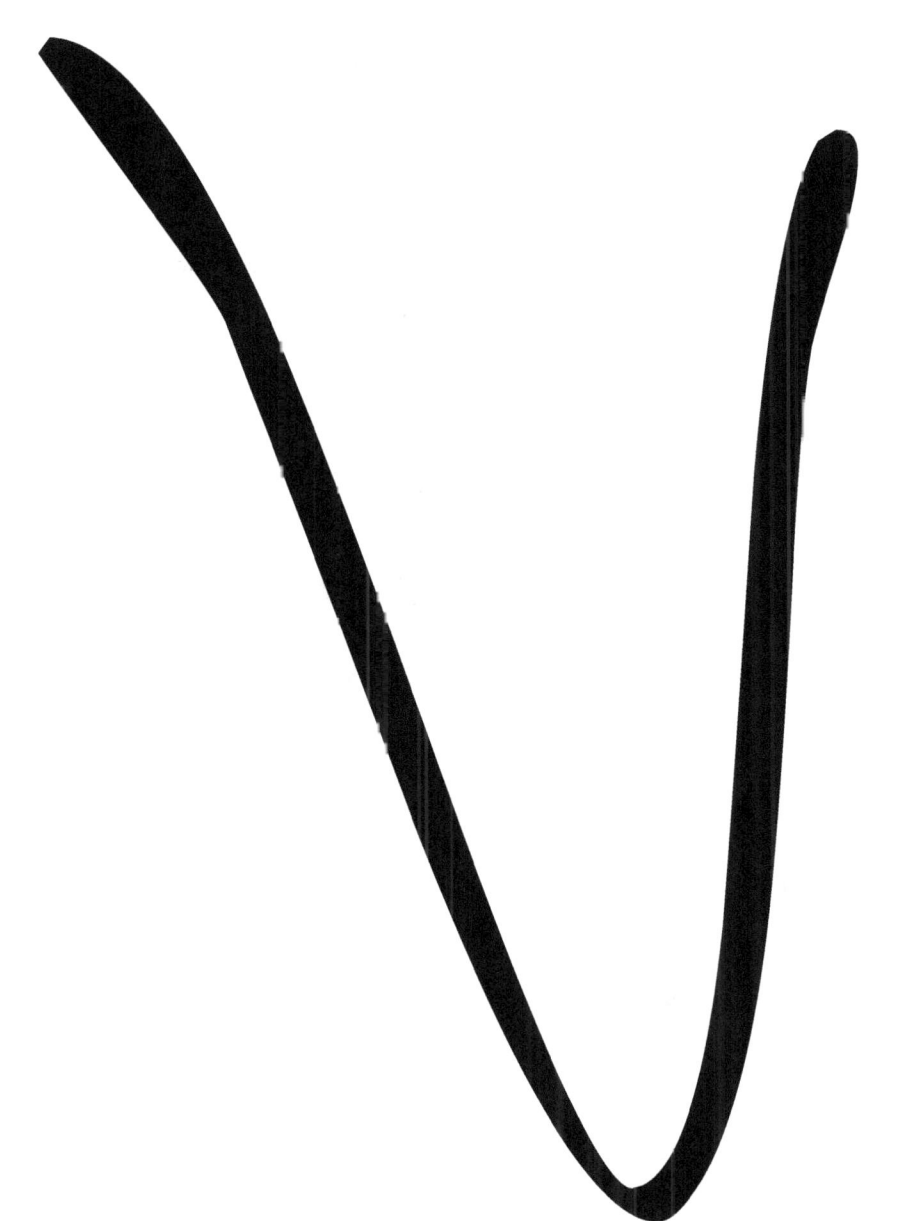

VEINS

To gaze at one's veins in a dream, is a threat of anxiety and trouble.

VELVET

Should you see some velvet dress or drapery in a dream, your luck will be good.

VERMIN

In a dream, vermin on your person or that of someone else, means luck and financial gain.

VERY THIN PERSON

A very thin person appearing in. your dreams, forebodes losses and troubles.

VEST-BUTTON

When a button drops from your vest, it is a promise of great success and prosperity.

VINE-PROPS

Those poles used to prop trees, vines, hops, etc., when seen in a dream, mesa quarrelling and disunion.

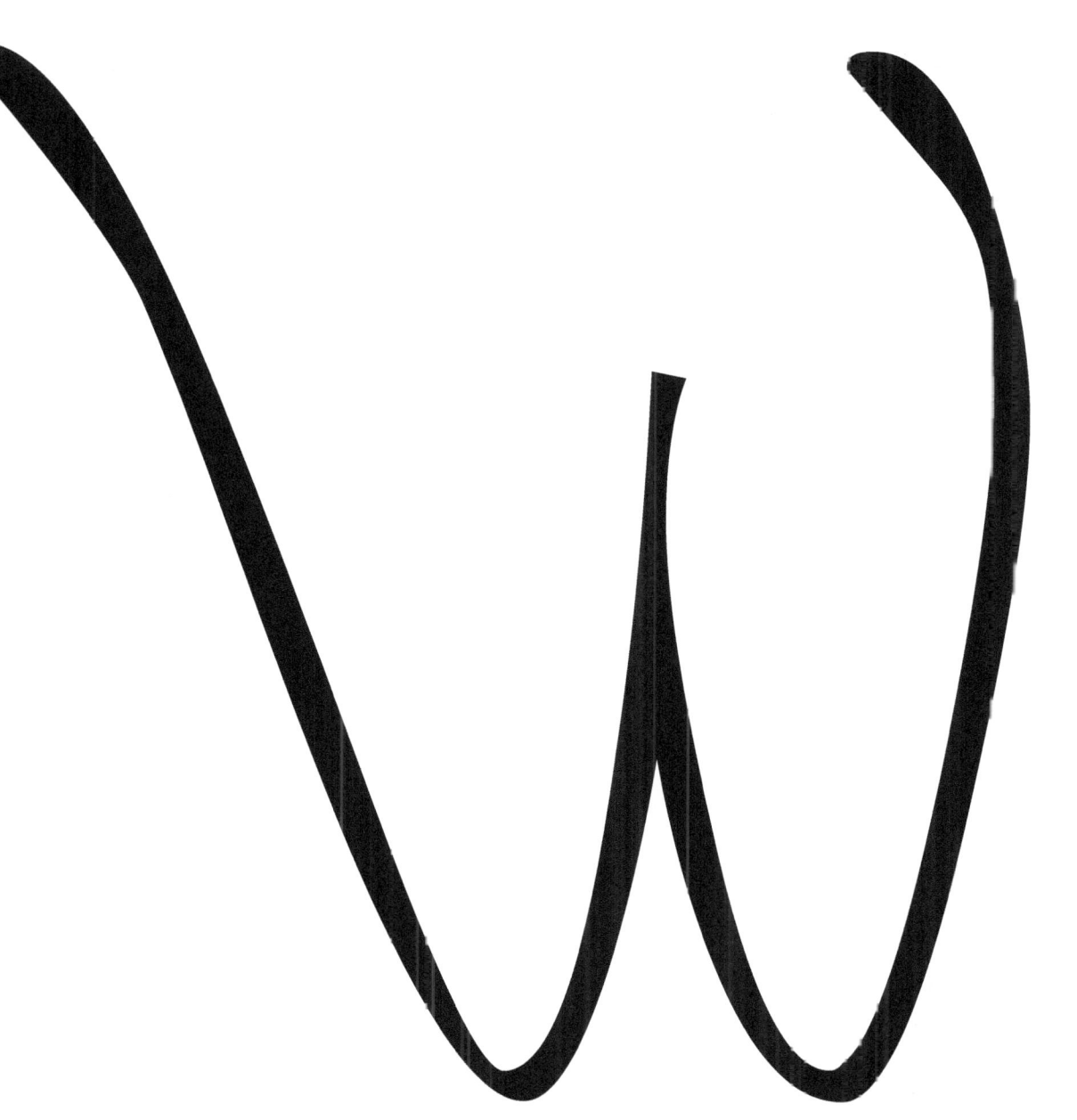

WALL

To dream of a wall is an omen of serious obstructions to your favorite plans: to see yourself upsetting it, is a promise of final success; but if you dream that you are building a wall, be assured that your labors will be in vain.

WARBLING

The warbling of birds, heard in a dream, is assurance of success.

WASH-BOWL

To dream of a wash-bowl announces coming inheritance.

WASHERWOMAN

It is a token of coming happiness to gaze in a dream upon a washerwoman at her work.

WEDDING-ATTIRE

For a maiden to try on, misfortune is imminent. If you are walking with someone else, sincere friendship will be yours; if it is a woman, you will soon marry.

WEDDING-DAY

To marry on a bright sunny day, is a strong omen of bliss; on a dark, rainy day, a threat of conjugal misfortune.

WEDDING

In a dream, to be present at a wedding is a threat of many troubles ahead.

WEDDING-RING

To dream of a wedding-ring means that your marriage is to take place very soon.

WEEPING

In a dream to see yourself weeping is a promise of great joys ahead.

WHEELS

An inheritance will soon to come to one who dreams of wheels.

WHISTLE

To hear a whistle in a dream is a warning of danger.

WIDOWHOOD

To dream you are a widow or a widower is a promise of some great satisfaction coming.

WIG

To see a wig, or wig-maker at work of a dream, means peril ahead.

WILL

To dream of your making your will is the saddest of omens; but if you see yourself writing someone else's will, expect much joy and satisfaction.

WINDOW

To dream of a window is an unlucky omen; it means quarrelling, misfortune financial ruin; and even imminent death if the window panes are broken.

WOODEN-SHOES

In a dream, wooden shoes signify final success after much hard, persistent work.

WOOL

To dream of wool means big profits in sight.

WORKMEN

In a dream, to see workmen at their tasks is a most lucky omen; if they are resting, you will soon be very poor; if they are fighting, a revolution is imminent.

WORK

To dream that you are doing some work with the right hand means personal good luck; if with the left hand, expect to be in straightened circumstances, for awhile, with final success however.

WORMS

To see worms or maggots in a dream, is a sign of illness coming.

WOUND

To dream yourself wounded gives promise of rapid advancement in your vocation.

THE

END

www.ingramcontent.com/pod-product-compliance
Lightning Source LLC
Chambersburg PA
CBHW081938170426
43202CB00018B/2944